The NAIS Head Search Handbook

A STRATEGIC GUIDE FOR THE SEARCH COMMITTEE

Second Edition

Vince Watchorn, Editor

ISBN: 978-1-63115-024-1
Printed in the United States of America

The National Association of Independent Schools provides services to more than 1,800 schools and associations of schools in the United States and abroad, including 1,500 nonprofit, private K–12 schools in the U.S. that are self-determining in mission and program and are governed by independent boards. NAIS works to empower independent schools and the students they serve.

To find out more information, go to the NAIS website at http://www.nais.org.

Editors: Susan Hunt, Myra McGovern, and Karla Taylor
Design: Fletcher Design, Inc./Washington, DC

National Association
of Independent Schools

Contents

SECTION A

CREATING A FIRM FOUNDATION FOR THE FUTURE

Looking inward, outward, and ahead, 7 ■ Understanding the school's leadership team, 8 ■ A scan of the environment, 10 ■ The school's vision, 12 ■ The individual who will lead the school toward that vision, 12 ■ The importance of diversity on the team, 13 ■ Ready to begin the search, 15

Six essential steps, 20 ■ The school's mission statement, 20 ■ Key questions and goals, 20 ■ Surveying and listening to all interested parties, 21 ■ Understanding education trends, 22 ■ Making sense of the data, 22 ■ Analyzing the data and developing a new leader profile, 23

Criteria for selecting the search chair, 25 ■ The chair's timeline and responsibilities, 26 ■ Two objectives of a successful search, 28 ■ Managing the process and working with stakeholders, 28 ■ Search committee, 29 ■ Board, 29 ■ Search consultant, 30 ■ Candidates, 30 ■ School constituencies, 30 ■ A unique opportunity to serve, 31

SECTION B

KNOWING YOUR OPTIONS, SETTING THE STAGE, AND STARTING THE SEARCH

SECTION D

EVALUATING SEMIFINALISTS

Acknowledgments

No work is done alone—we all stand on the shoulders of others.

First and foremost, I would like to thank NAIS President Donna Orem for the opportunity to explore through this volume the culture and salient issues of head search and transition today. In addition, thanks go to the 27 authors who made such important contributions to the book. We can all learn from each of them, and I very much enjoyed discussing their expertise on their chapter topic.

The following people offered thoughtful input that helped shape the volume in significant ways, for which I am thankful: Jim Bonney, Myra McGovern, Jay Rapp, Amani Reed, Kelsey Vrooman, Debra Wilson, and especially Karla Taylor. I am grateful, too, for the tutelage of Reveta Bowers, Dr. Peter T. Dalleo, and Peter and Karen Flint; the generous support of Ross B. Cameron Jr. and Catherine H. Cameron; and the unflinching confidence of Missie Watchorn Bauman.

This work is in memory of my mentor and friend, Edward J. Baker.

Vince Watchorn
Editor of the *NAIS Head Search Handbook*
Head of The Providence Country Day School (RI)
Winter 2018

Introduction

By Vince Watchorn

■ **In this book, a talented and experienced group of leaders from throughout the field help make sense of the search environment today.**

Gather virtually any group of veteran school heads and long-term trustees, ask what defines the head of school role, and you'll most certainly hear about how much—and how quickly—headship has changed. So many factors have contributed to this evolution: market economics, demand, branding, competition, technology, changing board perspectives and priorities, a growing sensitivity around interpersonal relations and the dynamics of inclusion, and more. There is today a greater need for schools to clearly define a compelling value proposition that, in many cases, brings pressure for a leader to deliver on specific, focused measurements of growth.

Just as headship is changing, so is search. Although the general process itself endures, a school today might take as much as 18 months or two years from the official announcement of a head's departure to the new leader's first day on the job. A board should approach search thoughtfully and strategically on any timeline, but that advanced calendar presents a near-luxurious opportunity to leverage search for institutional and strategic gain. A growing corporate search mindset is consistent with some trustees seeing the head's role differently. Costs are encouraging schools to be more creative or independent in their approach to transition. Psychological research and greater cultural awareness help the search process better reflect the values and realities of the 21st century.

Leaders are more than their interview performance. Some schools are taking advantage of recent research about hiring practices to study cultural competency and to observe action and track record rather than engaging in simple narrative exploration of candidate preparedness or falling for a cult of personality. These schools are trying to minimize the risk of falling victim to inherent bias by getting to know their candidates in broad ways; since the role of headship is broadening, so too should the way search committees explore candidates' talents. Many schools are trying to diversify their candidate pools, yet only some recognize that diversification is achieved most successfully as part of an overall culture of inclusion that extends into the search process—not as the start of such a culture.

Some schools choose to contract with a search consultant; others do not. For those that do, there is an ever-expanding pool of individuals and firms eager to take on this work. A wise school, of course, does not simply outsource its head search but hires a thought partner to coordinate this most important process for search committee deliberation. The more prevalent role of head as CEO and the potentially lucrative commissions from the independent school search market have attracted some corporate-focused search firms to join the group of boutique firms and retired heads who have led searches for so long. This has brought a new level of competitiveness and corporate mindset to identifying heads, and, more specifically, it has led to the concept of a closed-search model in some cases.

These issues and more are explored in this volume, *The NAIS Head Search Handbook: A Strategic Guide for the Search Committee.*

Here, a talented and experienced group of leaders from throughout the field help make sense of the search environment today. Collectively, they emphasize the strategic value of search to deliver the big-picture institutional perspective of how to maximize leadership transition for school improvement. They also review the nuts and bolts that might lead a search committee member to reach for this volume in the first place. After all, operating a well-coordinated, thoughtful search is a critical step in delivering strategic value. Together, these collected thoughts will help schools provide an intentional vision to find their next leader while also reaping the by-product benefits: a more engaged and galvanized community, improved communication, a greater culture of inclusion—and perhaps even a sense of shared leadership that could lead to effective succession planning.

Change is inevitable—in schools, in headship, in search. Amid this change, the thoughtful board and search committee will help their school make the most of leadership transition by understanding search in today's varied and evolving context. May you find not only a new leader but also the vision and momentum that will transform your school!

Creating a Firm Foundation for the Future

Making Room for Strategy

By Donna Orem

◼ Before becoming absorbed in the nuts and bolts of your school's search for a new head, you must devote time to looking inward, outward, and ahead.

Boards often approach the task of finding a new head of school tactically—asking what do we need to get done and by when. And there is, indeed, a significant amount of work to accomplish. The chapters in this book will cover all the key steps involved in the all-important task of finding a new head for your school.

But before your search committee digs in—even before deciding whether to hire a search firm or beginning to assess your school's need—we encourage the board to take a step back and make room for strategy and shared understanding.

To help you do so, in this chapter we'll make the case for the newly convened search committee to consider together questions like the following:

- Looking inward: What is the state of your leadership *team*? What strengths do you already have present on that team?
- Looking outward: What is going on in the world around you that has—and will have—an impact on your school?
- Looking ahead: What is your school's aspirational vision? And what kind of individual will be best equipped to carry it out?

Discussing these questions at the outset will help you develop a strategy for your search. It will also help the members of your search committee come to a shared understanding of what you are trying to do in the context of your school and the world in which you live.

■ The Power of Good Questions

In his book *A More Beautiful Question: The Power of Inquiry to Spark Breakthrough Ideas*, journalist and innovation expert Warren Berger makes the case that asking the best question is an art and a science, and that it will lead to the best answer. He brings to life many examples of people and organizations moving from the "Why?" to the "What If?" to the "How?" in addressing big issues.[1] As your committee crafts the initial questions that will guide your strategy, consider reading this book for inspiration.

YOUR LEADERSHIP TEAM

Your job as a board, through the search committee, is to identify the individual who will be the most effective head for your school. However, it's important to remember that this individual won't—and shouldn't—lead alone.

Before embarking on the search, your committee should learn about the dynamics of the leadership team already in place, including the strengths of the individuals who serve on the team. In most cases, the current head should be able to tell the board about these individuals. It's also helpful to come to a shared understanding in advance about the type of leader and leadership model that will best serve your school.

When you think of the school being led by a skilled team instead of one individual, it may change the way you consider the head's role. For example, many boards look for strong fundraising skills in a new head. But if there is a strong advancement professional in place, the skill you are more likely looking for in a new head is relationship building, not necessarily deep expertise in the tools and techniques of fundraising.

Undoubtedly, your school will be stronger with leadership distributed among various strong players. This model of distributed leadership may already be well thought out and documented at schools with strong succession plans, which the Bridgespan Group defines as "a proactive and systematic investment in building a pipeline of leaders within an organization."[2] If a succession plan is not in place, this is a task you will want the new head and board to consider down the road.

Recent research has shown the benefits to schools of distributed leadership, where leadership is shared and top leaders can focus on developing capacity in others. Bain & Company and the Bridgespan Group conducted research in 12 school systems nationwide. Among the findings detailed in their report, *Transforming Schools: How Distributed Leadership Can Create More High-performing Schools*, is that top leaders in schools often have supervisory demands that far exceed those of managers in other fields. School supervision expectations are onerous, if not downright impossible.[3] It's no wonder that school heads might find it difficult to focus on the larger strategic needs of the school. (It's also no wonder that many heads, especially new heads, often feel isolated and burned out.)

The same research also concludes that, although having a transformational leader at the top is critical, it is not enough. He or she needs to have a strong leadership *team* if the school is to be truly transformed and stay that way. The K-12 educational sector spends too much time waiting for "unicorns"—superhero leaders who can do everything—and not enough time developing leadership models that distribute leadership throughout the system. Even if the unicorn leaders make a difference, when they leave, the entire school infrastructure they created can fall apart.[4]

Also in support of a more distributed model of leadership is a 2008 study called *Ready to Lead? Next Generation Leaders Speak Out* that was produced by CompassPoint Nonprofit Services, the Annie E. Casey Foundation, the Meyer Foundation, and Idealist.org. The report profiles a leadership "crisis" in nonprofits. Three of four executive directors in the study said that they intended to leave their positions within three years, in large part due to inadequate compensation, burnout, and overwhelming fundraising responsibilities. The report points to dated power structures in which leadership is built around the concept of one individual or small group. These structures can lead to burden and burnout for these individuals and stifle the skills and creativity of others on the team. A new movement among nonprofits calls for a change from "individual-centered leadership" to "collective leadership." Supporters of this change cite evidence that this model can help nonprofits offer a better work-life balance, empower more types of mentorship and growth opportunities, and continue to attract and keep creative and mission-driven individuals.[5]

Given the multifaceted challenges of leading a school and the mounting evidence in support of distributed leadership in creating successful and sustainable educational environments, it's important to consider the *team* (current and

■ Millennial Expectations in the Workforce

Given their age and the sheer size of their generational cohort, millennials are either included in your leadership team now or will be soon. As a generation, they bring new passions, skills, and expectations to the job. As you assess your current leadership team and leadership model, consider generational trends such as these:

- Millennials are more diverse than any generation before them, and they expect diversity in their experiences.

- They want to collaborate and contribute toward a greater purpose.

- They want work-life integration and flexibility. In fact, the Annie E. Casey Foundation notes, "Gen X and Gen Y leaders ... may seek to restructure the executive role, creating collaborative or shared leadership models and job expectations that allow for a healthier balance between work and life."[6]

potential) before you launch your head search. If your school already functions with a distributed leadership model, then, during your head search, you need to consider whether candidates also support this model and whether their skills will enhance those of the current leadership team. Also, if your school employs distributed leadership, no doubt there are one or more strong internal candidates prepared to take on the headship role. If your school does not already use this kind of model, this transition could be an opportunity to move toward it.

The world of independent schools is growing more complex and demanding. Finding a hero leader is not realistic. So consider what kinds of strengths you already have on the leadership team, and begin to envision the type of head who can grow and lead the team into the future. And don't forget to consider whether that individual may already be in your school.

A SCAN OF YOUR ENVIRONMENT

To begin a head search with an informed and open-minded perspective—and to adequately represent to candidates your school's needs and positions—you need to be aware of the trends facing your school. Consider trends (including those specific to your local market) in areas such as the following:

Demographic Changes

Demographers predict that non-Hispanic whites will make up less than half of the country's population by 2044, if not before.[7] With this more diverse nation in mind, can your school move forward in a commitment to making the leadership, faculty, and student body more inclusive and representative of the whole country? What opportunities will you have to do so during this search?

Generational Changes

By 2020, more than one in three adults will be a millennial.[8] Millennials are now your school parents, alumni, and potential donors. How they view schooling, the debt they bear, their ingrained use of technology, and their desire for their children to be treated as unique should inform your school's enrollment and development efforts.

Changing Wealth Patterns

The wealth in our country has become increasingly stratified. As my colleague Amada Torres wrote in the *NAIS Trendbook*, "Participation in the labor force remains below pre-recession levels, and real wages have stagnated.... The recovery of the stock market has largely benefited high-income families, widening the gap between upper- and middle-income families."[9] In this context, many families, even some high-income families, may be questioning their ability to afford an independent school, especially as tuition increases have steadily outpaced wealth growth.

Having fewer full-pay prospective families is certainly a challenge for schools. Beyond the financial and admission aspects, it also makes committing to socioeconomic diversity and access even more complex in a tuition-driven industry. At the same time, research shows that education is the key to increasing mobility. These realities are important for your committee—and your new leader—to understand as your school seeks to live out its mission.

New Competition in Schooling

New educational options (in the public, nonprofit, and for-profit sectors) are emerging at a fast pace as teachers, entrepreneurs, parents, technology experts, and investors see new possibilities for improving student outcomes. New teaching and learning modalities that put students at the center of their education are birthing vastly different education models. This situation presents opportunities and challenges a new head will need to address.

No new head can be expected to come into the job with solutions to all of these complex challenges. But it's important that a candidate demonstrate an awareness of them and a mindset to address them. As for your search committee, having a general understanding of these trends will help you determine what kind of individual will most effectively lead your school into a fast-changing future.

YOUR SCHOOL'S VISION

In any strategic decision with school-wide impact (and a head search is certainly that), it helps to keep your eye on the bigger and longer-term picture. Your school has a mission statement that is important to keep at the center of the search, but your school's vision can give you that *longer-term picture*. Your vision is an aspirational statement, a "North Star," that reaffirms why your school exists and why you do what you do. It describes what your school envisions for its community in the future.

Turning to your vision at the earliest stages of your search process can help keep your committee focused and on the same page about what the school needs, not just today but also tomorrow. If your school does not currently have a vision, it may be worthwhile to develop a vision statement before beginning a head search. The following questions can serve as a guide for that process:

- What do you do best?
- What is your core capability?
- What needs can you satisfy that others can't?
- What kind of image do you want?
- What are your ethical and social responsibilities?
- What value do you want to have to your customers?
- What do you want to be in five years?

THE INDIVIDUAL TO LEAD THE SCHOOL TOWARD THAT VISION

With your future-focused vision in mind, your search committee can challenge itself from the outset to be open to candidates from both traditional and nontraditional sources. Recent research and thinking show the organizational benefits of doing so, especially in times of change.

Internal Candidates

Often in head searches, search committees overlook or dismiss internal candidates. These candidates may simply not be on the radar of the committee or the search firm the school hires. Or the committee may default to the importance of headship experience. Or the committee may inadvertently present obstacles that prevent internal candidates from being successful. For example, if searches don't allow for full anonymity, an internal candidate may hesitate to apply for fear of jeopardizing his or her current position.

In a 2015 article in *Independent School* magazine, Marc Levinson, who was then executive director of MISBO, questions several aspects of the "old way" of conducting head searches, including this reluctance to hire internally. He writes,

> In 2013 and 2014, approximately 80 percent of the new CEOs at the top S&P 500 firms were hired internally. These people were carefully groomed and selected to lead their organizations. It is essentially the opposite at independent schools, in which somewhere in the neighborhood of 85 percent of heads are hired externally.[10]

Levinson sees this as a major missed opportunity, especially in light of the number of baby-boomer heads who are stepping down and given that we are at a moment of great change in education.

> As the number of retiring heads increases over the next five years, boards may need to change their principle of hiring an experienced head. Also, given the current widespread transformation in education, it may be that the "experienced" heads are not able to bring the skills, innovation, and creativity to the job that they brought in the past.[11]

Although comprehensive succession planning cannot happen retroactively at the time of the search, your search committee must understand the growing importance of fully considering internal candidates.

Diverse Candidates

By and large, boards want their leadership to reflect the diversity of their school and of the country. As an industry, however, we have struggled to achieve this important goal.

NAIS research shows that the share of female heads at NAIS schools has hovered around one-third since the turn of the century. The share of heads of color has ticked up from only 3 percent in 2000-2001 to 7 percent in 2015-2016. NAIS studies also show a confidence gap between men and women: Sixty-six percent of male aspiring heads of color said that they are highly confident in their ability to become head of school, compared with 43 percent of women of color and 43 percent of white women.[12] In research conducted with members of NAIS's Aspiring Heads cohorts, women reported believing that a glass ceiling exists for them, which may contribute to that lack of confidence.[13] In a study on gender diversity conducted by the American Association of University Women (AAUW), the term "labyrinth"—as coined by Alice Eagly and Linda Carli in their 2007 research on the topic—is used to describe the complex nature of the barriers to women's advancement.[14]

Further, there's a noticeable disconnect between the qualities that search firms and committees seek and what women and people of color *believe* these firms and committees are seeking. For example, candidates said they thought "experience at a similar school" was the least important qualification, but search firms valued this highly. Similarly, candidates did not rank "prior experience as head" as highly as search firms and search committees did.[15]

In your school search, consider how you can address these types of disconnects to keep your search fair and open to all of the best possible candidates.

Nontraditional Candidates

Bill Durden, former president of Dickinson College and a presenter at the 2016 NAIS Leadership Summit, makes the case that educational institutions should also remain open-minded about leaders who haven't followed a traditional leadership track or perhaps don't even come from an educational institution. He supports the notion that these individuals could make the best leaders in times of change because they experience the institution from outside the norm, giving them a heightened clarity and focus. He explains that because they are given

■ Research Shows Teams Are Most Effective When They Represent Gender Diversity

When researchers at the University of Maryland and Columbia University studied top firms in the Standard & Poor's Composite 1500 list, they found that gender diversity equated not only to innovation but also to better financial results. The study also found that companies that prioritized innovation saw greater financial gains when women were in top leadership positions.[16]

no road map, have no "traditions to defend," and never quite belong in the social and professional context in which they have arrived, they may feel a greater sense of comfort with change.[17]

In higher education, there is disagreement about the value of hiring nontraditional candidates—those who didn't come up through the usual faculty ranks. *Inside Higher Ed* reports that "data from the American Council on Education's *American College President* study found in 2011 that just 20 percent of college presidents had come to their jobs from outside academe, and more than half had never worked anywhere *but* in higher education." Those who support continuing to hire from within academia believe that the cultural gap and knowledge of values are too important to forgo. On the other hand, college and university boards are increasingly considering hiring nontraditional candidates in the hope that they will take bigger risks and bring greater financial acumen and strategy to the job. Others conclude that whether the candidate comes from within or outside academia, a search committee should focus on the school's specific goals and the traits of the individuals who can best meet those goals.[18]

Starting an independent school search with an open-minded perspective—and with the school's specific goals and vision as the highest priority—is certainly a strong foundation from which to attract the widest breadth of candidates. Such a mindset will improve both the search itself and the ultimate outcome.

READY TO BEGIN THE SEARCH

Once your board has considered and come to agreement on the issues this chapter raises, your search committee will be equipped with a shared understanding of your school's current leadership dynamics and the leadership model that will fit best. Your scan of the environment will give you context about a more diverse population as well as changing customers, shifting workforce, and emerging competition. And your school vision will compel you to look to the future.

As you begin to take the steps necessary to find your next head of school, you can be confident that the search will be comprehensive, open-minded, future-focused, and strategic.

ENDNOTES

[1] Warren Berger, *A More Beautiful Question: The Power of Inquiry to Spark Breakthrough Ideas* (New York: Bloomsbury, 2014).

[2] The Bridgespan Group, "Building Leadership Capacity: Reframing the Succession

Challenge," 2011, p. 2; online at https://www.bridgespan.org/bridgespan/images/articles/building-leadership-capacity/BuildingLeadershipCapacity.pdf?ext=.pdf.

[3] Chris Bierly, Betsy Doyle, and Abigail Smith, *Transforming Schools: How Distributed Leadership Can Create More High-performing Schools* (Boston: Bain & Company, 2016); online at http://www.bain.com/Images/BAIN_REPORT_Transforming_schools.pdf.

[4] Ibid.

[5] Simon Mont, "The Future of Nonprofit Leadership: Worker Self-Directed Organizations," *Nonprofit Quarterly*, March 31, 2017; online at https://nonprofitquarterly.org/2017/03/31/future-nonprofit-leadership-worker-self-directed-organizations/.

[6] Tim Wolfred, "Building Leaderful Organizations: Succession Planning for Nonprofits," The Annie E. Casey Foundation, 2008, p. 5; online at http://www.aecf.org/m/resourcedoc/AECF-BuildingLeaderfulOrganizations-2008-Full.pdf.

[7] Sandra L. Colby and Jennifer M. Ortman, "Projections of the Size and Composition of the U.S. Population: 2014 to 2060," U.S. Census Bureau, March 2015; online at https://www.census.gov/content/dam/Census/library/publications/2015/demo/p25-1143.pdf.

[8] Fred Dews, "11 Facts About the Millennial Generation," Brookings Institution, June 2, 2014; online at https://www.brookings.edu/blog/brookings-now/2014/06/02/11-facts-about-the-millennial-generation/.

[9] Amada Torres, "The Economic Outlook," *NAIS Trendbook 2015-2016* (Washington, DC: National Association of Independent Schools, 2016), p. 7.

[10] Marc Levinson, "Advanced Placement," *Independent School* magazine, Spring 2015.

[11] Ibid.

[12] Ari Pinkus, "A Call for More Inclusive, Empathetic Leadership," *Independent Ideas* blog, November 8, 2016.

[13] NAIS/Insightlink Communications, Aspiring School Heads Longitudinal Study, 2008/2009 Cohort, March 2013 (unpublished), and NAIS/Insightlink Communications, Aspiring School Heads Longitudinal Study, 2007/2008 Cohort, February 2012 (unpublished).

[14] American Association of University Women (AAUW), *Barriers and Bias: The Status of Women in Leadership* (Washington, DC: AAUW, 2016).

[15] Pinkus, "A Call."

[16] Katherine W. Phillips, "How Diversity Makes Us Smarter," *Scientific American*, October 1, 2014; online at https://www.scientificamerican.com/article/how-diversity-makes-us-smarter/.

[17] Bill Durden, Presentation at the NAIS Leadership Summit, October 2016, Baltimore, Maryland.

[18] Doug Lederman and Scott Jaschik, "Race on Campus, Nontraditional Leaders, Rising Confidence: A Survey of Presidents," *Inside Higher Ed*, March 9, 2016; online at https://www.insidehighered.com/news/survey/race-campus-nontraditional-leaders-rising-confidence-survey-presidents.

1. At the outset, set aside tactical considerations and develop a strategy for your search. The strategy should be rooted in a shared understanding of what your board and search committee are trying to accomplish in the context of your school and the world at large.

2. Look inward at the state of your current leadership team to gain an accurate sense of what strengths your school already possesses. This will help you determine the kind of head of school you need to grow and lead the team.

3. Look outward by scanning likely changes in demographics, generational traits, wealth patterns, and your competition.

4. Look ahead at your school's aspirational vision and the kind of individual who will be best at leading the school toward that vision.

5. With this vision in mind, be open to internal candidates and ones from both traditional and nontraditional sources.

Here and on other pages throughout the book, "Advice From the Field" provides additional insights into the head search process. The contributors include heads of regional independent school associations and search consultants.

Think creatively. Search committees are often so worried about getting their search wrong that they fail to take the leap that would get the search right.

Clay Stites, President, Resource Group 175

Keep in mind that it's not about you. Remember that you are serving the board and school, not your own idea of what the next head of school should be.

Jake Dresden, Senior Search Consultant, Carney, Sandoe & Associates

Organize for success. Before making any key decisions, provide trustee education about the requirements of a successful search process, including the right search chair, committee composition, and requisite lead time. This will also give you the foresight to think strategically about the qualities needed in the next head of school for this particular time in history.

Rhonda Durham, Executive Director, Independent Schools Association of the Southwest

2

Assessing Your School's Needs

By John E. Creeden

■ Your school, your board, and your candidates all benefit when you invest time in an accurate, candid needs assessment.

Independent schools need different kinds of leaders at different points in their history. For example, the leadership skills that a startup school requires change once it's established and operating smoothly. Similarly, when a once-prosperous school faces challenges with financial sustainability and enrollment shortfalls, it needs a leader whose skill set specifically matches the community's current needs.

That is why the departure of your head of school, whether planned or sudden, offers your board and other leaders a rich opportunity to reflect. It's the ideal time to conduct a thorough analysis of the state of your school, consider critical questions, and have essential conversations about the future. What you learn will be invaluable in two ways:

You will sharpen your focus on what you need in your future leader. After all, there may be many qualified candidates in a pool. But the essential question is, "Which candidate will be the best fit for *this school* at *this time?*"

You will also be ready to give candidates an accurate and comprehensive picture of your school. Remember: The integrity of the search process and the reputation of the school are best served when the board is transparent about the most critical issues. As in all cases, honesty is the best policy. You want your candidates to feel confident that what they see and hear from the search committee is an accurate depiction of current conditions.

If your board members have done everything possible to understand your school's current strengths, weaknesses, and challenges, then they can be confident they're searching for a head of school who can meet those challenges.

SIX ESSENTIAL STEPS

As explained in the section on vision in Chapter 1, it's essential for your board to maintain a sharp focus on why your school does what it does and on what it needs to realize the future it envisions for itself. So that your school can articulate its motion forward and the leadership characteristics that can best deliver on its vision, your board should develop a needs assessment. Here are six steps to consider.

1. Start with the mission statement.

Your school probably displays its mission statement prominently in everything from its hallways to its website. But what role does the mission statement truly play in your school's plans for both the future and day-to-day operations? Is there broad agreement on what it means and how it is incorporated into the curriculum (that is, all that you do with intention)? Has the board recently reviewed and endorsed the mission? Does the board, along with the faculty and students, use it to guide its deliberations and decisions?

2. Develop key questions and goals.

The departure of your head of school may not naturally coincide with a comprehensive process of thinking strategically about the future. In fact, organizing a strategic plan may be one of the tasks you intend to assign to your new head of school. But whether or not a recent strategic plan is in place, your board should know the answers to the strategic questions in the following list.

Admittedly, the board is not responsible for supervising a number of the listed areas, such as curriculum and faculty recruitment. However, your board members should be aware of the answers, or the lack of them, when responding to these questions as they construct the profile of the next head of school. Since nothing in an independent school happens in isolation, it should be obvious to your board that the questions are interconnected and vital to a proper analysis of the current state of your school.

- Does the school have a clear statement about the goals of the curriculum (again, all that you do with intention)?

- Has the admission office collected data on recent enrollment and demographic trends, and does it have specific goals for addressing any concerns?
- What analysis has been done to assess short- and long-term financial sustainability?
- How does the school define, measure, and promote diversity? Has the school recently conducted any research to assess it?
- What measures does the school use to assess the quality of faculty and staff, and what strategies are in place to recruit and retain qualified individuals?
- How effective is the development office in generating annual and capital support across multiple constituencies?
- Does the school have a campus facilities assessment and master plan for the future?

3. Survey and listen to all interested parties.

One of the differentiating characteristics of independent schools is the relational nature of teaching and learning in our communities. That is, it's not only the quality of the curriculum that matters but also the close relationships faculty and students develop that promote increased student learning. If your board members understand and embrace this concept, then the board must reach out to faculty and staff, alumni, parents, students, and other individuals who are part of the school and ask for their feedback.

In recent years, the formal search has become in many cases a highly confidential process. Advocates of the closed-search process feel that by limiting participation to the search committee, schools can attract candidates who wouldn't apply if news of their interest might leak to their current employers. In contrast, involving constituent groups early on in the search by asking for their opinions doesn't just open up the process. It also provides constituent data to guide the search.

To collect such data, boards may decide to sponsor open meetings for interested parties to attend in person, or they may use electronic surveys. In either format, you should ask questions such as the following:

- What do you see as the current strengths of the school?
- What is critical for the school to do better as it seeks to improve?
- What do you see as the future direction of the school?

- What skills should the next leader of the school possess?
- How can the search process best serve the school's goals as the search begins?

4. Become familiar with national research and discussions about education trends that affect your school.

Your trustees need to be aware of the conversations that thought leaders in education are having so they can compare their school to what's happening across the country and around the world. For example:

- What are the critical issues in intellectual and social-emotional development in early childhood education, middle school, and upper school?
- What are the trends in risk management, learning and teaching, and tuition cost controls?
- What do thought leaders see as the most pressing issues affecting finances, demographics, faculty/staff recruitment, and environmental sustainability?

Whether you're conducting a regional or national search, your board also wants to represent the school as being current with today's best practices in education. That means becoming familiar with best practices across multiple topics. A good way to start is by reviewing the NAIS Principles of Good Practice at http://www.nais.org.

While conducting this analysis of trends and best practices, your board needs to keep the mission statement close at hand and assess where there is congruency with what's happening in other schools. Being true to your school is important both for the analysis your board is conducting and for the potential pool of head of school candidates.

5. Make sense of the data.

Sometimes boards have a tendency to rush to judgment and then act hastily based on what they learn from surveys, recent studies, and open forums. Your board should stop, pose a series of questions, and make sense of the data before deciding what to do, says Cathy Trower, president of Trower and Trower, Inc., a consulting group that works with nonprofit boards. According to Trower, boards should focus on what the data tell the leadership group about the school, its culture, and the way various constituent groups see its current and future state.[1]

Above all, your board should avoid the temptation to use the data to affirm preconceived notions of what your school needs. This kind of confirmation bias can lead you to look for information to support what you already believe and discount evidence that conflicts with your beliefs.

6. Analyze the data and develop a new leader profile.

This profile (which you can read more about in Chapter 7) should be based on feedback and identification of the range of leadership skills the next head of school needs. Your board is responsible for collecting the answers to the key questions and then assessing major strengths and weaknesses. Many board members have completed SWOT analyses (strengths, weaknesses, opportunities, and threats) in their professional lives. The rationale for collecting data in the for-profit sector is equally sound in an independent school. Your board should share this information with candidates, who will want to know what's going well and, more important, where improvements are needed.

When approached carefully and with a clear set of objectives and strategies, a needs analysis can help your board see the period before the search process publicly begins as an opportunity for growth. Accurately assessing and describing the current state of your school is the first step to a successful search.

ENDNOTE

[1] Cathy A. Trower, *The Practitioner's Guide to Governance as Leadership: Building High-performing Nonprofit Boards* (San Francisco: Jossey-Bass, 2012).

1. Start with your school mission. Does your mission statement describe the school's highest goals? Does your board support the current mission statement?

2. Develop key questions. For example, what are your school's strengths and weaknesses now? Where does your school see itself in the future?

3. Collect data and feedback from key constituents. Be as inclusive as possible.

4. Be familiar with national research and discussions about key education issues. What are the best practices?

5. Make sense of the data you gather before taking action. What do the data tell you about your school, your culture, and what constituents think?

6. Formulate a new leader profile based on an accurate assessment of collected data. Be true to your school and honest with candidates.

3

Choosing the Search Chair and Getting Started

By Laura Ryan Shachoy

▪ The search chair has two key objectives: to help the search committee reach a unanimous decision on a candidate for the board's approval and to involve stakeholders so they see the process as fair and well-managed.

Without question, serving as search chair can be labor-intensive and demanding. But it is also deeply rewarding. The process of hiring a new head will have a lasting impact on your school community and can be one of the most productive exercises a board tackles. It offers the opportunity to make an impact while giving back to the school in a unique way.

An outstanding search chair and dedicated search committee are key to shepherding the school through the process of selecting a new head. Once the board appoints the chair and committee, their charge is either to recommend one candidate to the board for its approval or to provide two finalists for the board's selection. The former practice is by far the most common. After all, the search committee is most familiar with the candidates and the school's needs and thus in the best position to recommend one stellar candidate.

The importance of the task warrants careful consideration to ensure that your school selects the search committee's leader carefully, based on a keen understanding of what the role will entail.

CRITERIA FOR SELECTING A SEARCH COMMITTEE CHAIR

As with other board committees, the executive committee or board chair names the search committee chair or co-chairs. Although no written rule prohibits your board chair from also serving as search chair, it is advisable for someone else to oversee the search since the board chair already faces substantial demands on her or his time. However, given the board chair's critical role, as well as the close working relationship between the head of school and board chair, your board chair should be a fully participating member of the search committee.

When choosing your search chair, your board should select an active and engaged trustee who is respected by the school community. Every search is different, but it is usually desirable for the search committee chair to become the successor board chair and occupy that position when the new head arrives. If that's not possible, it is important for your search chair to be connected at the upper levels of your school's institutional discourse.

As Donna Orem writes in Chapter 1, above all, the search chair must commit to looking inward, outward, and ahead. The chair must guide the committee through an examination of the state of the current leadership team, the many trends affecting your school today and tomorrow, and a compelling school vision. That commitment to arriving at a search outcome that will truly prepare your school for the future is vitally important.

The following attributes are also helpful for carrying out the search chair's myriad duties:

- Deep knowledge of your school culture and a sound understanding of your school's strengths and challenges
- Reliability and willingness to devote the necessary time and energy to lead the search
- Strong organizational and communication skills to coordinate and plan meetings, interviews, and candidate visits as well as to connect with the school constituencies
- Skills in meeting management and interpersonal relations and an appreciation for the collaborative work necessary for a successful search
- The good judgment to balance two crucial components in the search process: confidentiality and transparency
- A good working relationship with the board chair

THE SEARCH CHAIR'S TIMELINE AND RESPONSIBILITIES

Opinions differ about the point at which your school should engage a search firm (if a firm is deemed necessary). Some believe that the board chair should lead the selection of the consulting firm and, since philosophies differ from firm to firm, wait to select the full committee until after the consultant is secured. This way, the board chair may ask the search chair to select some or all of the remaining committee members. However, others believe strongly that this sequence will cause your committee to feel less invested in the process. They recommend that the search committee form first, take ownership of the search strategy under the search chair's direction, and then choose the firm that can best help enact that strategy.

The search chair's public role begins with the announcement to the school community of the search committee membership and its chair. The role continues through the conclusion of the search with the public announcement of the new head. During this time, the search chair is involved in many critical decisions. These include whether to conduct an open or closed search; whether the search should be elongated or abbreviated; and whether the school should retain an interim head so you have ample time to be thoughtful and thorough about the selection. (Read more about interims in Chapter 5.) There are no right or wrong decisions. They depend on a variety of factors unique to your school's culture, needs, and specific strengths and challenges. But your board should expect the search committee chair to be central to these conversations and to communicate the rationale to the full community.

Serving as a search chair requires a substantial commitment of time and energy throughout the process. But the most demanding periods are usually at the outset, when the chair is assembling the search committee, establishing the search process calendar, and preparing a position statement, and at the end, when finalists are visiting campus. If you're working with a search firm, the search chair will often get a reprieve while the consultants are developing the applicant pool. But if your board decides not to retain a firm, your search chair's time commitment and responsibilities will continue to be heavy as he or she leads the committee in all aspects of the search, including gathering input, creating the position statement, and developing a candidate pool.

The search chair can also play a valuable role beyond the close of the search as the new head joins the community. The chair is a familiar face to the new head, is well-versed in the new head's background, and—one hopes—has developed a rapport with the new head through the hiring process. So, it makes sense to involve the search chair as a member of the transition team. If the search chair cannot serve, another search committee member should be included.

OBJECTIVES OF A SUCCESSFUL SEARCH

As the saying goes, it is helpful to begin with the end in mind. That is why your search chair must remain focused on two key objectives:

1. **To reach a unanimous decision on a candidate to bring to the board for approval.** Unanimity sends a powerful signal to the board, which will in turn, everyone hopes, also cast a unanimous vote. The board's unqualified support will bolster the new head's successful introduction to the community and smooth the transition.

   Here's an important point to emphasize: *The search chair's role is not to determine who will be the next head of school.* Rather, it is to work diligently to create and maintain a collaborative, respectful, and professional atmosphere so the search committee can achieve the necessary consensus.

2. **To inform and involve stakeholders so they view the process as fair, thorough, and well-managed.** This short-term objective has long-range implications. The search chair must engage the school community to muster as much support as possible for the board's choice; instill confidence in board leadership and the process; and, generally, encourage buy-in. Although the head selection is strictly within the board's purview, the choice of a new head is always enhanced by honest feedback from the perspective of the school constituencies. For more on this topic, see Chapter 4 on engaging the school community in the search process.

   The challenge is to maintain the balance between transparency (which ensures that your community perceives your process as fair, comprehensive, and well-run) and the need to protect the confidentiality of committee deliberations. Frequent communication of appropriate information to the community is critical to achieving this balance.

MANAGING THE PROCESS AND WORKING WITH THE STAKEHOLDERS

As the project manager, the search chair must keep many balls in the air. The tasks include leading the search committee deliberations, scheduling meetings, updating school constituencies, working with the search consultant, interacting with the candidates, and presenting the final selection to the board for its approval. To accomplish all this, the search chair works closely with the following groups and individuals.

The Search Committee

As mentioned before, the search chair's role is to guide the search committee to a consensus on one candidate who is the best fit for the school culture and most capable of leveraging the school's strengths and facing its challenges. Establishing a collegial, collaborative, and respectful atmosphere within the committee is paramount. In addition, the search chair must ensure that committee members have all relevant information and remain focused on the school's mission, culture, strengths, and challenges as well as the type of new leader the board and community envision.

The search chair is ultimately responsible for all search process communications, meetings, and interactions with the search consultant and candidates. However, the search chair may delegate some of these duties to members of the search committee. They may take ownership of tasks, such as maintaining the schedule, managing travel and lodging, and stewarding on-campus visits.

However, the chair may also get such help from other sources. If you're working with search consultants, they may handle many logistical tasks as well as communications. Or you may appoint a reliable and knowledgeable school employee to act as a search liaison. A natural choice is someone who regularly deals with sensitive information, manages important school communications, is familiar with scheduling logistics, and has the trust of the community. Of course, it is imperative that such a liaison understand the need for complete confidentiality.

The Board

The most important collaboration between the search chair and the board is to establish goals for the search and a vision for how the committee will work to achieve those goals. This requires the kind of strategic thinking outlined in Chapters 1 and 2.

On a tactical level, it is essential for the search chair to provide the board with a clear timeline and framework for the search process and to update board members frequently. This means providing status reports at regular board meetings and periodic updates by email as necessary between meetings. Again, confidentiality is critical, but the board should have no doubt that the search chair is accessible throughout the process for any questions or feedback.

The search chair also sets up meetings for board members to speak to finalists when they visit campus. Board members then provide their feedback in writing to the search committee.

The Search Consultant

Most search chairs are novices. If your school decides to hire a search firm, a seasoned consultant can provide valuable insights based on years of experience. The consultant can be a resource to both the search committee and its chair by providing support through every step. The search chair works closely with the consultant and communicates often on the phone or by email.

Consultants can help with a multitude of tasks. These include gathering information from constituencies for the school's assessment, assisting in the preparation of a position statement, helping devise a search strategy, advising on issues that arise during the process, and offering additional information and perspective on candidates' backgrounds and qualifications. Consultants are often available to assist during the transition period as well. Learn more about consultants in Chapter 6.

Head of School Candidates

If you're working with a search firm, your consultants may be your candidates' chief point of contact. If you don't engage a firm, the search chair may be the person who sets up candidate interviews and campus visits for the finalist candidates. Because the chair enjoys regular contact with the candidates, he or she will have a unique window into their interpersonal skills and will be able to provide additional perspective to the committee on how they might fit into the school culture.

The search or board chair notifies the semifinalists and finalists of the school's decision. It's important to send thank-you notes to candidates who will not be advancing further in the process to express appreciation for their time and interest.

School Constituencies

In many respects, the search chair operates as the face and voice of the board to the school community. The search chair is responsible for driving all communications regarding the search process. These include meeting announcements and website postings, answers to inquiries, and community updates by letters and emails.

As you'll read in Chapter 4, there are a number of ways to gather feedback from your constituents. Many schools find that they can get the most useful input from surveys with key constituent groups. Some use advisory committees whose ranks are drawn from faculty and staff, past or current parents, alumni, or close friends of the school. No matter how you handle the feedback step, your search chair needs to make sure that it is carefully managed as part of the larger strategic process so that you don't complicate matters without adding much value. In particular, you want to make sure that your constituents understand that the search committee will always be the only group with all the information that ultimately influences a decision. It's important not to inadvertently establish an "our choice" versus "their choice" mentality. Otherwise, the search result could be called into question by the community and undermine the new head's stability.

Of course, a change in leadership virtually always creates ripples in the school community. Your search committee and its chair can, through effective communication, manage community expectations and offer reassurance that the school is moving in a positive direction. Frequent communication from the search chair provides the inclusiveness and transparency that assures the community that the process is well-run, fair, and comprehensive. Such communication also instills confidence in the board's leadership and invites the community's engagement in the process. It is the best way to let the school constituencies know how and when they will have opportunities to add their voice to the process.

Although the selection of the head of school ultimately rests with the trustees, the school constituencies' input about the school's core strengths and areas for improvement and their vision for new leadership is important. The search chair's engagement with school constituencies and the way the chair handles their input are critical to the search's success.

Here's a final note about the search chair's work with all stakeholders. It is important to underscore that the search process is a two-way street. While your school is assessing the candidates, the candidates are evaluating your school. All individuals and committees must remain mindful that they are serving as ambassadors and can influence the process for good or ill.

A UNIQUE OPPORTUNITY TO SERVE

A successful search can mean more than simply choosing an outstanding new head of school.

For the board, it encourages trustees to revisit and recommit to the school's values and mission, and it also spurs generative thinking.

For the school community, a well-managed process can be energizing and affirming; it's a chance to celebrate the school's strengths, and it lays the foundation for understanding and meeting the challenges ahead.

For the search chair, the demands of the role are offset by its deep rewards. Serving in that role gives a trustee the opportunity to make an impact while giving back to the school in a unique way. In addition, it develops and strengthens relationships with fellow trustees and within the school community.

During this demanding process, search chairs should thank fellow search committee members often and acknowledge the value of their time, commitment, and talent. A celebratory dinner or gathering at the end of the process is a thoughtful way to express well-deserved appreciation for the members' hard work. Such an event provides closure to a demanding and time-consuming process while recognizing the importance of the committee's endeavor. It also celebrates the camaraderie that is likely created throughout the search process.

1. Remember that effective communication is key. Keeping the community well-informed throughout the process will go a long way toward minimizing any anxiety that the search process and a change in leadership can bring.

2. Understand that a successful search balances transparency and confidentiality. Although it's important to communicate with the community throughout the process, leaks concerning the search committee work and the candidates' identities can compromise the integrity of the process.

3. Never forget that the search process is a two-way street. It is the search chair's responsibility to inform the search committee and other school constituencies of their dual roles as evaluators and ambassadors.

4. Stay positive. The search chair's optimistic outlook sets the tone for productive search committee work and can help alleviate some of the natural apprehension that arises in the community.

Putting Strategy to Work

By Karla Taylor

■ **Smart search committees devote more time to soul searching than to shopping for candidates.**

It's one thing to understand what thinking strategically means in principle. It's another to put it into practice. To give your search chair, search committee, and board a concrete sense of how strategic thinking applies to a search, here's advice from two longtime educators who have experienced the process from both the candidate and committee sides.

Avoid the urge to zero in on candidates immediately.

"Too often, strategic thinking goes out the window because search committees are thinking about shopping as opposed to strategy," says Wanda M. Holland Greene, head of The Hamlin School (CA). "They see the process as searching for a product instead of making a strategic match."

So don't start out by asking where the best candidates are and how your school can get them. Instead, "Stay away from candidates as long as you can," she says. Reverse the arc of the search from the usual—20 percent soul searching and 80 percent shopping—to 80 percent soul searching and 20 percent shopping.

Put another way, Holland Greene says, "Spend time preparing the soil instead of looking for seeds to plant."

Let the timeline be a guideline, not a mandate.

Holland Greene tells of search committee members who, to meet a self-imposed deadline, forced themselves to choose from three finalists they weren't convinced were right. The result was "a really big mistake."

She recommends that your committee make a promise to itself: You will not sacrifice your school's needs and desires on the altar of a timeline. Then the committee needs to convey the message to the school community by saying, "We're going to do this job and do it well, but at end of the day, we are not going to let time be a chokehold." Making this clear from the start will reduce anxiety in your community.

Think critically about your search committee's composition.

Recruit individuals for the committee who understand and have experience with the hard business of hiring, says Katherine G. Windsor, head of Miss Porter's School (CT). Don't use the committee to represent every conceivable constituent group, reward the capital campaign chair, or let the faculty and staff choose their new boss.

Conduct a thorough self-study.

In their rush to find candidates, too many schools plunge into writing the position description without taking the time to reflect on their true needs. The result is a bland sameness that's familiar to anyone who compares head of school position statements, says Windsor.

The strategic alternative involves a rigorous, and rigorously honest, self-examination. Among the probing questions to consider about your school:

- Who are you, and what do you really need in a new leader? When Holland Greene was considering her position at Hamlin, she was impressed by how thoroughly and candidly the search committee had thought through the school's need for curricular improvements and a campus master plan. As with dating, she says, it's better to be frank to avoid unpleasant surprises.

- What is the state of your market—demographics, economic prospects, competition—and how are those likely to change?

- Why would someone want to be your head of school? Avoid the assumption that great candidates will recognize your school's greatness and clamor for the job. Instead, examine and articulate your institutional strengths and challenges. "You need to assume that nobody knows about you, and it's your job to tell your story," says Holland Greene.

Read more about self-examination in Chapters 1 and 2.

Be hard-headed about your school's situation.

Too often, Windsor says, candidates move through the search process believing what starry-eyed search committees tell them about their schools' circumstances. "Then they get there on July 1 and the reality is completely different. They find out the classes aren't full, the budget isn't balanced, and the neighbors are unhappy about parking." The near-certain result: a head who's disillusioned by July 31.

Most search committees aren't deliberately dishonest. Instead, there's a disconnect between the kind of person the school needs and the process the school follows to get that person.

Search committees often overlook the reality: "Independent schools are a business with huge compliance issues, such as safety and legal issues," says Windsor. In such cases, neither the position description nor the interview process will tell the prospective head that "you don't spend your time on soccer fields. You spend your time with lawyers, PR people, and dealing with HR matters."

A strategy-minded board will avoid the pitfalls of focusing on these aspects:

- *Omnipresence.* Don't obsess about finding candidates who'll pledge to sit in on every class, soccer game, committee meeting, bar mitzvah, and alumni happy hour. Even if such magical ability to be everywhere exists, that doesn't make them good heads.

- *Teaching experience.* "There are amazing candidates that too many schools won't look at because they haven't been teachers," says Windsor. "Saying you can't be a suitable school leader if you haven't taught before is like saying you can't be an airline CEO unless you've been a flight attendant or a pilot."

- *A likeable spouse or partner.* Concentrate on whether candidates can lead the school to the future the board envisions, not on whether the significant other is really nice. As for including the spouse or partner in interviews: "That's crazy," Windsor says.

Remember that the search firm works for your school, not the other way around.

Especially when the committee chair is not an educator or is inexperienced with recruitment, "there's sometimes a tendency to defer to the search consultant and say, 'You think this person is great for us? Well, OK then,'" says Holland Greene. "The search chair should hold the vision of the school in his or her heart and keep pushing the search consultant to find not just more candidates but the right match for that vision."

Fight bias.

The candidate with the best skills to enact your school's vision may not look like his or her predecessors. "When schools say they want diversity, they must be willing to really examine their thinking about who they want to lead their school," says Holland Greene. "I wish for the day when anti-bias training is built into every search process." Read more about counteracting the role of bias in Chapters 9 and 10.

Reassure the community.

If you're going to think strategically about your search timeline, committee composition, and qualifications for the ideal head, you also need to think strategically about how to convince the school community that this approach is in everyone's best interest.

Start by explaining that your committee will communicate, but only when there's news, not constantly. When you do communicate, speak of "our search," not "the board's search." Remember that your school is like an orchestra, with everyone playing together under the direction of an attentive conductor—the search committee chair.

Finally, win respect for a strategic search process by framing it positively. "A fierce optimism needs to exude from the pores of the search committee, and especially the search chair," Holland Greene says. Every communication should convey excitement about opportunities in a time of change. "That doesn't mean fear will never creep in," she says, especially if your former head left under less-than-desirable circumstances. "But say, 'We *get* to do this—not we *have* to do this.'" After all, your search is the chance to find the leader who will put down roots and truly inspire your school to grow.

Understand who's in charge. To gain the maximum value from the search, the search chair—not the consultant—must lead it. The search chair must learn the process, build a strong team, and guide the process through to a successful conclusion.

Marc Levinson, Principal, Independent School Solutions, and former Executive Director of Mid-South Independent School Business Officers (MISBO)

Work as a team. Be honest, open, discreet, collaborative, willing, supportive, engaged, and positive.

Ben Bolte, Senior Search Consultant, Carney, Sandoe & Associates

Be receptive to others' opinions. Second only in importance to maintaining confidentiality is seeking consensus. One member of a search committee can throw a wrench into the process by sticking doggedly to one point of view regardless of others' entreaties. Consensus also makes the work much more rewarding because you learn so much from others.

Peter Philip, Search Consultant, Carney, Sandoe & Associates

Start strong by engaging each person. Every search committee member should feel like an active part of the process, not a passive bystander. At the first meeting, the chair should ask everyone for a contribution, perhaps when discussing essential characteristics or brainstorming about identifying top candidates. Be sensitive to interpersonal nuances that may prevent full participation. Hearing from each person lays the groundwork for a robust process.

Robin Tweedy, former Senior Consultant, Carney, Sandoe & Associates

Knowing Your Options, Setting the Stage, and Starting the Search

4

Engaging the Community in the Search Process

By Deirdre Ling and John Mackenzie

■ From the announcement of the head's departure through late-stage meetings with finalists for the job, the search is an opportunity to bring the school community together to take stock and get excited about its collective future.

Changes in leadership, whether after long periods of stability or short intervals at the helm, are major inflection points for schools and their stakeholders. It is a widely accepted principle of organizational behavior that change is most successful when those affected are involved in the change process.

Even though hiring a new head of school falls within the purview of the board of trustees, a well-managed search can be an important opportunity for your entire school to take stock, build community, and prepare for the change to come. A potentially anxiety-provoking event can be transformed into a time to build a collective vision of a bright future based on a celebration of your school's strengths and an honest assessment of its challenges. Only by understanding who and where you are as a school can the members of your community—including faculty, staff, parents, students, and alumni—collectively articulate what they believe your school needs in its next leader.

There are two major times during the shift to new leadership when community involvement is especially valuable.

AS THE SEARCH BEGINS

For your community at large, the transition starts once news of the current head's departure becomes public. That first official communication sets the tone for the process that will ensue. Generally, the announcement is a dual one from the head and the board chair. The fact that it is a joint communication underscores the partnership between head and board. It celebrates the school's achievements during the head's tenure and allows the board chair to express thanks for the head's accomplishments and service. It also provides information on the steps the school will undertake to ensure a smooth transition of leadership. Done correctly, the communiqué is the first step in engaging the school community going forward in a spirit of collaboration and transparency.

Often, by the time the board and head are ready to make a public announcement, school leaders will have already made decisions about several important facets of the search. For example, the board may have appointed a search committee or may allude to the fact that the committee and its members will be announced soon.

Deciding how to involve the community in the search committee

Some believe that because the responsibility for hiring and employing the next head of school lies with the board of trustees, the search committee should be made up mostly or entirely of current and former trustees. Others see the search committee as an opportunity to engage various constituencies and find it beneficial to include a few faculty, staff, parents, or alumni. Although these individuals can bring useful perspectives, including them may raise political questions about why some were chosen and others were not—and any resulting controversy could break down the community you seek to build. Ultimately, the best search committee configuration will depend on your culture and circumstances.

Fact-finding for the needs assessment and position statement

A major step in signaling that community engagement matters is to undertake a needs assessment grounded in honest feedback. The assessment may use surveys, focus groups, information analysis (contained in, for example, an existing strategic plan or recent accreditation report), and one-on-one conversations to take stock of how key constituents perceive the school. An anonymous and confidential gathering of this information will produce the truest understanding of the kind of leader your school needs and help you develop an accurate position statement. (See Chapter 2 for more on the needs assessment and Chapter 7 for information on profiling the position.)

Think carefully about how to make sure that the feedback you get is both honest and broad-based. Confidentiality can be crucial. Members of the school community are more likely to speak candidly when asked to identify themselves as part of a particular constituency rather than as individuals. In addition, it is important to take this opportunity to reconnect with disengaged community members through individual outreach. Doing so allows your search committee to benefit from the opinions of the disengaged while making them feel valued because the school has sought out their insights.

Once the findings have been used to inform the position statement, many schools make the statement available publicly, often on a special section of the website designed to update the community on the search from start to finish. Sharing the position statement openly enables everyone to have a common understanding of the characteristics the school is seeking in its next head and the tasks that lie ahead.

Informing and reassuring the community

In any search process, it is a challenging balancing act to provide transparency about the process while simultaneously offering confidentiality to and about candidates. From the start, state openly that the search committee is committed to both. Letting the community know that there will be a quiet phase as you post the position and recruit and vet candidates assures everyone that the process is on track. Because this quiet phase can sometimes last for months, the search chair should provide periodic updates to reassure your community that your search is progressing smoothly.

AS THE DECISION NEARS

Again, your search is likely to yield a stronger pool of candidates if you can protect their confidentiality until very late in the process. Unless schools opt for the closed-search model, in which none of the candidates are public other than the candidate of choice, most searches will protect the confidentiality of all candidates except for the small group of two to five individuals selected as finalists.

When at last the finalist stage arrives, a process that has mostly taken place behind the scenes becomes public. As this public phase nears, the search committee should inform community members about how and when they may be involved, most likely by meeting finalists who will be invited to campus. This further expands the opportunities for community input and engagement.

There are different ways to meet the candidates and provide feedback, depending on the degree of inclusivity your search committee thinks is appropriate to your school's culture.

Meetings enable stakeholders not only to take the measure of candidates but also to hear each other and the varying viewpoints that enrich the fabric of your school community. Meetings can take place among the head's direct reports, key academic and administrative leaders, faculty, parents, past parents, alumni, and community leaders. They may occur in larger forums, in small groups, or one-on-one. Allowing the candidate to meet with larger groups of faculty and staff, as well as with parents and alumni, has two benefits. Members of the school community can become acquainted with the candidate. Members of the search committee can also observe the candidate's presence in front of larger groups—an essential aspect of headship.

Advisory committees are an additional way to involve the community at the finalist stage. This model is probably most appropriate for larger schools, where it is often difficult for individuals other than trustees and senior administrators to have concentrated time with candidates during a very full visitation schedule.

The most effective advisory committees range in size from 12 to 20 individuals and include a mix of constituents, such as faculty, staff, parents, and alumni. This mix will enable committee members and candidates to gain a broader perspective about the school's future leadership needs. But as the committee's title indicates, it is essential for this group to understand that its role is only to *advise* the search committee on its impressions of the candidates. Advisory committee members offer feedback based on each individual candidate, not as a ranking or statement of preference. Your search committee should draft any kind of feedback forms carefully to encourage the right kind of input.

During the finalist visits, members of your school community should keep in mind their roles as both buyer and seller. Just as the school is trying to determine which candidate is the best fit, candidates are assessing their level of interest in the position. Each candidate may also be grappling with the larger question of whether the extended community is the right fit for a spouse or partner and family. To put its best foot forward as a seller, the school can benefit from involving volunteers in tasks such as hosting, answering non-school questions, entertaining, and, when needed, even providing a local real estate introduction.

■ What Is the Current Head's Appropriate Role?

Except in circumstances where the current head's departure has been disruptive, there is more to be gained by having the current head involved with rather than removed from the search process. Inevitably, people will ask about the current head's impression of the process. It is much more beneficial if the head can answer, "I have been kept up-to-date and believe the process is going very well," rather than saying, "I have no idea."

Your current head's broad knowledge of your school, other schools, and what it is like to go through the search process can be invaluable to your search committee, consultants, and finalists. As a result, it is appropriate that the current head share perspectives on the school with the search consultants and with finalist candidates. That said, it must be clear to both the current head and your community that the head has no role in selecting the new leader.

Gathering the late-stage feedback in productive forms

Those who meet the candidates during the finalist visits should have an opportunity to provide the search committee with their feedback. In most cases, it can be best to do this through an anonymous survey. Survey questions should be open-ended and broadly stated: "What do you perceive to be the strengths of this candidate?" "What further questions or areas do you think the search committee should explore with this candidate?" "Please feel free to offer any thoughts or observations about this candidate."

If you are working with a search firm, typically your search consultants receive survey responses online via a link provided to respondents. The consultants may provide a "live" link to the members of the search committee to view responses, or they may sort the responses for the search committee by constituent groups. Sorting by constituent groups often provides valuable insight into how a candidate is received by specific constituencies as a whole even though each individual responds independently.

Survey data are valuable for many reasons. The results offer community perspectives at the critical stage when the search committee is narrowing the choice to a handful of candidates, any one of whom might be an excellent next head of school. The information provides an additional data point for the search committee to consider before making its final recommendation. The findings also remind individuals who take the time to complete the survey that their opinions will be considered in the spirit of inclusivity, as promised at the beginning of the search process.

Sometimes it may also be appropriate for the search committee to get in-person feedback from key individuals; for example, on occasion, the search chair may meet one-on-one with the head's direct reports to gain impressions related to their specific areas of expertise. Once again, just as at prior points in the process, search committee members should be clear that they are asking only for input.

That brings us back to a point that cannot be overemphasized. Even with broad community involvement, the ultimate responsibility for the selection of the next head of school belongs to the board of trustees acting on the search committee's recommendation. That's because those groups, and especially the search committee, will have information not available to others. The search committee will have garnered perceptions of candidates from multiple constituencies, completed confidential reference and other background checks, and spent considerable time with the candidates. This kind of measured and inclusive process puts the committee in the best possible position to select a leader who meets the carefully identified needs of the school at this particular point in its history.

The search for new school leadership is the best opportunity for your board of trustees to position the school well for future success. If it is thoughtfully organized and well-led, the search will result in your school community being unified around a head of school who knows the challenges and will provide strong leadership during a rewarding tenure.

1. Recognize that, if managed correctly, the head search provides the school community with an excellent opportunity to determine its future paths and the qualities of leadership best suited to help the school move forward.

2. Keep in mind that even though the ultimate responsibility for choosing a new head of school lies with trustees, the trustees can

benefit significantly from the input of others about what they seek in a new head and how they respond to meeting finalist candidates.

3. Realize that the search committee is responsible for keeping the school community well-informed about the search process and progress. It also has an equally important responsibility to maintain a high degree of confidentiality. Thoughtfully balancing these two considerations will have a profound impact on the success of the search for your new leader.

5

Considering an Interim Head of School

By Charles F. Clark

■ In their haste to find the next head, boards may be tempted to view "interim" as a negative state. However, by carefully choosing an interim leader, you are likely to accomplish a great deal in preparation for the long-term head's arrival.

Successful interim heads of school are like experienced maritime pilots. Interim heads are valued for their knowledge of how to board the ship that is the school and navigate it into a safe harbor, thanks to their understanding of the treacherous waters that may lie ahead. Like maritime pilots, they are given full responsibility for the ship, its cargo, and its passengers—students, parents, faculty, administrators, trustees—who may be unaware of the threats from rocks, sandbars, swirling currents, crosswinds, and passing ships.

Also like maritime pilots, interim heads know that even though they are on board for only a short time, they can never take their eyes off the destination—or the long-term effects of what they do.

By thoroughly considering the possibility of appointing an interim, your school increases its chances of avoiding an unexpected—and unnecessary—crisis with less-than-adequate leadership at the helm. You may engage the interim to help manage specific issues, such as potential restructuring or program review, or simply to bridge the gap between a long-term leader and a new one. Whatever the circumstances, an interim may be able to help navigate your school safely through the waters ahead.

HOW DO YOU DECIDE WHETHER AN INTERIM IS RIGHT FOR YOU?

To answer this question, your board members should consider the following:

- Does the school have an adequate succession plan in place?
- Does the school have an acknowledged, capable, and primed internal candidate ready to take over? (If so, you may already have your likely interim. Read more about internal interims later in this chapter.)
- Is the current head's resignation being announced before November, when there is still likely to be a good pool of candidates?
- If the school has been evaluated for accreditation in the last three to five years, has the board stayed on track with achieving the goals of the strategic plan that may have grown out of that experience?

If the answer to most or all of these questions is no, then your board should strongly consider an interim head for the following school year. Here's why.

Hiring an interim for a year or more helps you manage the paradox of school change.

The paradox dictates that the board must move forward with a sense of urgency while remaining calm, cool, and deliberate as it considers its present challenges and best future. As noted in Chapter 1, it's vital to take the time to discuss the hard questions that will help you develop the proper strategy for your search. In a time of imminent change, this can be difficult when board members face a rush to judgment by constituents demanding that the board expedite the search for the "right" head of school. The phenomenon is often exacerbated by board members' own fear of failure and concern about looking anything less than responsive to stakeholders.

Unfortunately, there are many cases that illustrate the negative effects of boards acting precipitously. Your board members need to remind themselves that they are responsible for creating room for strategy and shared understanding. They are also making a major monetary investment with a payoff that is likely to last for the next eight to 10 years. They should take the time to fully consider the consequences of any decision. Therein lies the paradox of change: You must move forward quickly but only after the entire board has participated in thoughtful and meaningful deliberations.

Timing is everything.

It's important to conduct your search when there is a critical mass of head candidates available who fit your school's mission. The optimal time to search is late spring, summer, and fall of the year before you want your new head to start. The worst time is late winter or early spring when you need a new head for the next school year. When heads give notice in the weeks or months after Thanksgiving that they will depart the following July 1, one possibility is for schools to begin to search without delay, realizing that the field of eligible and available candidates is rapidly narrowing. School leaders can keep the interim option in mind, knowing that if they can't find appropriate candidates for the permanent position, qualified interims will still be available in late spring. Another possibility is to choose the interim option immediately so there will be a full search cycle for seeking the ideal successor head.

An interim may also be a wise choice if a promising candidate is employed in another school and can't be available immediately.

The right interim is more than just a placeholder.

The interim serves as a bridge between the past head of school and the next permanent head—a connection that helps reduce anxieties, allows time to build confidence in the search process, and encourages the school to focus on its future. In addition, the right interim may be uniquely capable of the following:

- Helping the community adjust to the loss of a beloved longtime head of school
- Identifying and troubleshooting problem areas
- Developing strategies for future initiatives that shouldn't wait
- Improving and implementing specific operational systems
- Executing current plans
- Addressing pressing needs
- Educating the community on governance and coaching administrators and emerging leaders

If entered thoughtfully, an interim period will be a time when some of your school's most important work can be accomplished.

HOW DO YOU FIND THE RIGHT INTERIM?

Let's say the conditions are right for appointing an interim head of school. As mentioned before, if you have a primed internal candidate, your problem may be solved. But, if a capable candidate is not available, your next objective is to decide whether to choose a search firm to help you find the right interim.

In brief, it can be advantageous to work with consultants because of their breadth of understanding of what's involved in conducting a search and leading a school. Also, search firms are likely to have lists of interim specialists or candidates of interest who are available on short notice. The disadvantage is that you can't expect consultants to have a deep-seated understanding of your school's specific culture.

If your board chooses not to use an outside consultant to find your interim, you should follow a process similar to the one you'd use for a permanent head search. Under the guidance of a search committee ranging from four to nine board members, you need to create a position profile, advertise the position, screen and interview candidates, and conduct careful reference checks on your finalist. However, if you're hiring an interim late in the year or in an emergency, the tight time frame may dictate having a smaller committee, a less elaborate position description, a more expedited (but *always* thorough) candidate review, and a more nimble decision. An extended interview process may have to give way to a leap of faith regarding the choice(s) available.

WHAT SHOULD YOU LOOK FOR IN AN INTERIM?

Tops on the list of characteristics to search for are professional and emotional intelligence; multiple experiences in a headship or an interim role (unless the person is an internal candidate); relational acumen; and well-developed communication skills. Next is the ability to read situations quickly and adroitly in order to retain discipline around the essence of a school in the process of change. Last, but not least, is the facility for lowering anxiety levels by collaboratively engaging school leadership in the work and openly supporting the staff.

If nothing else, an interim's wide array of on-the-job experiences should give the board the confidence it needs to not only identify problems but also to find the right next head who will be in a position to solve the school's problems in the future.

Thoughtful and deliberate boards can fairly quickly recognize potential interims' areas of strength and weakness that match the school and then substantiate their judgments with thorough reference checks. When choosing finalists, search members should focus on the strengths that best match the school's phi-

■ What to Consider When Hiring Your Interim

Desired traits:

1. A high degree of emotional intelligence (as verified in references)
2. Ability to coach and communicate effectively with administrators
3. Understanding of the diverse leadership styles and qualities necessary to provide a bridge in the short term and create a workable leadership team for the long term
4. A multitude of perspectives drawn from a variety of firsthand experiences with understanding and solving problems similar to ones your school faces
5. Added value from past interim experiences and a good reputation
6. Ability to achieve instant credibility without carrying excessive baggage to the school

Personal operative strengths:

1. Ability to demonstrate a good fit between the individual's core beliefs and the school's cultural core values
2. A leadership style that is appropriate to your school and that is collaborative and positive
3. Ability to connect quickly with the community
4. Ability to gain the confidence of the school's leadership in the first three months
5. Ability to laud teaching excellence immediately on recognition
6. Wisdom to inquire about board expectations but refrain from setting long-term goals outside the scope of the interim position
7. Ability to identify potential problems and blind spots by mid- to late fall of the interim year and to work with the board to address them in the near term as needed and appropriate

Particular problems or needs your school would like an interim's help with:

1. Political situations your community is facing, either now or on the horizon
2. Specific issues affecting the school, both in the next year and in the long term

Keep in mind that it's vital to be open and honest about the challenges your school faces and what you expect from the interim.

losophy and needs in strict order of importance. Careful matching should provide the school with a very good choice.

A final consideration is vital but often neglected: a detailed transition plan. This plan should include appropriate meetings with board members, staff, major donors, parents, and alumni. Although board members may need to be more involved in maintaining critical external relationships during the interim year, the interim head must understand that this kind of individual outreach is a vital part of the job.

The transition plan should extend beyond the interim's year of service; after all, the interim is passing the baton between two heads, not just taking it from the predecessor. With this layer of thoughtful planning, the interim is better positioned to adequately implement the strategic plan or the particular strategic charge for which the individual was hired.

WHAT DOES AN INTERIM COST?

Compensation should be commensurate with the interim's experience and skill set and aligned with the school's compensation philosophy. Too many schools see hiring an interim as a way to save a few dollars by lowering the salary. Hiring an interim should never be about money, and the interim should be compensated fairly. What a school receives from the right interim will be far more valuable than just the fiscal investment. Remember, you are hiring an experienced specialist to carry out specific strategies, not a baby sitter.

There may be cases in which a school would like to keep an interim for an additional year. To avoid causing confusion, cynicism, or both, don't wait to consider this possibility until you're in the middle of the search. Decide this either before you start the search for the permanent head or after the search for the permanent head fails to produce the proper candidate. In addition, determine in advance whether your interim is eligible to apply for the permanent position.

WHAT IF AN INTERNAL CANDIDATE COULD SERVE AS THE INTERIM?

Hiring a current staff member to serve as interim comes with its own benefits and challenges. A major benefit is that an internal interim would already be culturally adjusted and would understand the school's political and internal roadblocks. The person would also provide consistency. This could be extremely valuable if your most recent head's departure was due to some form of upheaval and change would be difficult for the staff and school.

In addition, in some cases an internal candidate will receive significant support from staff and unanimous support from the board of trustees. If so, the internal interim could be in an excellent position to become your next head of school.

The downsides are most evident when the school faces significant changes in the near future. An internal interim who aspires to the permanent position may not act as quickly on needed changes related to staff or programs. That's because such changes invariably cause some community upset and could ultimately work against this interim's prospects. In addition, if the internal interim has no headship experience, the individual may be less capable of managing the bumps in the road during the transition. In such cases, the board needs to be prepared to support the interim with training and executive coaching.

More often than not, a groundswell of support emerges among staff to make the internal interim the permanent head. Depending on the school's state and size, board members may feel that, to stabilize the school, they must ultimately appoint this person. Despite the pressure, board members must look carefully at the internal candidate and come to an objective conclusion about whether this person is likely to have the long-term skills and support to succeed in the permanent position.

On occasion, the internal person may unexpectedly express a desire to be considered for the permanent job while the first half of the search is in process. Too often, boards take this quick way out rather than extending the search. However, only in highly unusual circumstances should you change the ground rules and cut short your transparent, predetermined search process. If you've already informed the community that a search will occur, the search should continue as planned with the participation of the internal interim candidate.

The internal interim's contract can be a good tool for ensuring that you stay within the agreed-upon parameters. With the help of a school lawyer, you can make sure that the internal interim's letter of agreement and contract both spell out the specifics of the transition to the permanent position. The contract can also detail the steps to take in the event that the interim would like to be considered for the long-term position. A legitimate process is both a necessary step and a best practice when you're in the middle of the most important change your school will go through. Taking a thorough, responsive approach will ease anxieties and curb speculation.

NAVIGATING TO SAFE HARBOR

Returning to our opening analogy, always bear in mind that the chief benefit of having the equivalent of an experienced maritime pilot is that the individual will steer the school through unfamiliar waters. An interim can help you guarantee a safe journey until the new captain, or head of school, comes on board. If all goes well, the members of your community will be able to look back and say, "The interim head of school piloted us through many unexpected situations. Without that person's insight and help, we would not be as far along as we are today."

Ship ahoy, mate!

1. Recognize that your school can accomplish important work under interim leadership.

2. Review the current condition of the school and the immediate challenges ahead. Consider the interim option in the first conversation your board has after learning that your head will not be returning for the next school year, especially if the head gives fewer than seven months' notice.

3. If your school is unconvinced about the value of an interim and tempted to dismiss the concept out of hand, talk with your search consultant and other resources to understand the true value of an interim step—and the potential costs of a hurried search.

4. If you choose an interim, be sure that your school's leaders understand specifically what they want the interim to accomplish. Clearly articulate these expectations to the interim verbally, in goals and objectives, and in the interim agreement

5. View your interim as a professional specialist rather than a baby sitter or source of salary savings.

6. Remember that the degree to which you involve the interim in the search process is a board decision—unless the person is determined to be a candidate from the start, in which case the interim should not be involved in the decision-making process.

6

Choosing a Search Firm

By Claudia Daggett

▨ The process of selecting a search firm requires asking numerous important questions, including who makes the choice, when to get started, and what determines the fees.

You will read frequently in these pages that hiring the head of school is, arguably, the board of trustees' most important responsibility. As many authors note, you must plan to invest your time and the school's resources wisely to get the best result: the right person to lead your school at this point in its evolution.[1]

In this chapter, we'll explore the advantages of using executive search counsel for this important process; roles, timetable, and strategies for selecting the right consultant; and key differentiating factors among search firms. Even if your school chooses not to secure a consultant for your search (see page 67), this chapter could help you understand the work you will need to conduct on your own.

WHAT CAN A FIRM OFFER THAT YOU CANNOT DO YOURSELF?

It can be tempting to forge ahead without a search firm, especially when resources are tight, the last search was recent and the process well-documented, or if your school is perceived to be outside of the norms or mainstream of independent schools. The case for enlisting the help of a firm lies in the services listed below, which consultants are uniquely positioned to provide:

Guiding the school through the process

Having shaped and adapted an approach based on experience with a number of schools, search consultants will recommend a set of important steps. They will advise you about the composition of your search committee, develop a search calendar and communication plan, and help you stay on track with your timetable. Most important, they will help you anticipate the typical hiccups and points of tension along the way and find the best remedies to address them.

Seeing the school's needs from an outside perspective

In addition to meeting with the search committee, strong search consultants will spend time in the school observing classes and other school activities and interviewing students, faculty and staff, parents, board members, and graduates. Consultants can combine this experience with knowledge of an array of independent schools. Then they can offer your board and search committee observations in context; identify any systemic issues your school should address before the new head arrives; and convey to candidates, accurately and compellingly, the position's opportunities and challenges.

Leveraging knowledge of prospects beyond the immediate school and community

Search consultants report that as much as one-third of their candidate pools comes from direct recruiting of individuals who are not actively looking for new positions—recruiting based on consultants' knowledge of comparable schools and promising individuals. Ideally, they do so by drawing on relationships they've built over time with current and aspiring school leaders. Another third of the candidate pool typically comes from referrals from colleagues: heads, association directors, and others in the field. The final third consists of applicants who respond directly to a position statement or advertisement.

For your pool of candidates to be both robust and diverse, consider leadership potential from a broad range of sources beyond your school community and beyond those who have self-identified. Consultants can be the key to this breadth. Chapter 7, about profiling the position and building the pool, articulates this in detail.

Preparing the search committee for interviews

Your search committee is, most likely, made up of volunteers, some of whom may not have experience with interviewing for hiring. Consultants can coach you in this area. They can help you create meaningful, open-ended questions to get a good sense of your candidates in the short time an interview allows and make you aware of the kinds of questions you must avoid to ensure an equitable and legally sound process. Consultants also may help you interpret what you hear in interviews.

Researching the candidates

Often, consultants do some initial checking of references. Perhaps most helpful, they may offer guidance in identifying "unofficial" references—individuals who have worked directly with the candidate but are not on the reference list. Consultants may also conduct the necessary background checks or point you in the right direction to complete this step on your own.

Assisting in closing the deal and managing transition

Many firms will help you determine whether the compensation package you intend to offer is sufficiently competitive and help you bring the negotiations to closure. It is important to determine what role you want your consultants to play in determining the compensation package, especially if the search fee is based on first-year salary. Consultants also can be very helpful in guiding your committee through the details of discussing compensation—particularly when to broach the subject with candidates and how to conduct those conversations.

If a candidate is participating in other searches simultaneously, consultants typically will discuss this directly with your prospective head of school and work to manage the timetable so you make your offer in time to land the person of your choice.

In addition, many firms offer guidance on the process of welcoming and acclimating the head of school after you make the appointment. Some consultants include follow-up meetings with the head of school and board during the first year. If this interests your school, you might discuss at the outset what transition services you hope your consultants will provide.

WHO CHOOSES THE SEARCH CONSULTANT?

Most often, the board chair is the individual who will identify the trustees best suited to shepherd the search. The board chair will act in consultation with other board leaders, often in the form of the executive committee. From this point, different schools may take different approaches to forming the committee and selecting the consultant. The trustees who make up the preliminary search leadership group may be the ones who form the search committee in its entirety; or they may simply be the group that gets the process started; or they may be the initial members of the search committee, with others to be added later, after the consultant is in place. To distribute workload and prepare for long-term board leadership succession, the search committee chair is often the person most likely to serve as the next board chair. The search chair also is likely to lead the process to select the consultant.

As discussed in Chapter 3, some schools believe that it's important to fully form the search committee before engaging the consultant. To maximize buy-in, all committee members first work together to develop the search strategy under the search chair's direction. Only then do they choose the consulting firm that they believe can best enact that strategy.

At other schools, the preliminary search leadership group selects the consultant. Most often, the search committee chair leads the selection and keeps the board informed of the process; the board chair participates from this point forward on an ex officio basis. Because search consultants vary in their advice about ideal search committee composition, school leaders who decide not to pin down the committee configuration and search strategy at the start remain flexible about these matters until the consultant is on board. Some consultants may suggest a committee made up exclusively of trustees, perhaps with advisory committees of other constituent groups. Others may suggest a more inclusive configuration with members drawn from trustees, parents, graduates, faculty, administration, and other friends of the school.

Whether the full board votes on the group's recommendation for a consultant or delegates this decision to the group depends on the board's policies and practices for a decision of this type. (However, when it comes time to approve the search committee's recommendation for the new head of school, the full board votes.)

The consulting firm will present a letter of agreement outlining the timetable, fees, and other details. Then an official representative of the school—usually the board chair—will sign that agreement.

WHEN DO YOU GET STARTED?

In the early 2000s, nine to 12 months was a reasonable amount of time to mount and complete a search. A process would begin in the late summer or early fall, and an announcement would be made by early December, with the new head to begin the following July. As sitting heads announced plans for new appointments, a second wave of searches would take place that concluded in the late winter or early spring. Today, for many schools, the desired window is 18 months, with the appointment made a full 12 months before the new head's start date. This shift, presumably due to an increasingly competitive market, has created an additional earlier wave.

With that in mind, you should get started, at least in a quiet phase of the work, as soon as you know that you have a leadership position to fill.

If you're replacing a long-term head of school or have had an abrupt departure, you may consider appointing an interim head of school first. You can read about interims in detail in Chapter 5. If you choose to pursue an interim, get your consultant in place first if possible and lean on counsel to help you identify and transition to the interim. Some firms will conduct the interim search as part of their fee for the full process.

WHERE DO YOU FIND OUT ABOUT FIRMS?

You can choose from a number of different sources of information about search consultants.

- **NAIS.** As of this book's publication, 20 executive search firms were listed in the NAIS online directory, and more than a dozen others engage in the work on occasion. You'll find the current list at http://www.nais. org > directories > find a company > executive leadership search.

- **Organizations that specialize in higher education.** A number of independent schools, particularly large boarding schools, have moved to using firms focused primarily on clientele in higher education. Academic Jobs, a higher education employment site, offers an extensive list of executive search firms at http://www.academicjobs.net/academic_search_firms.php.

For recommendations on consultants that have served schools like yours, consider taking these additional steps:

- Contact peer schools that have recently conducted searches.
- Reach out to your regional independent school association executive for recommendations.

- Subscribe to *The Blue Sheet*, published by Educational Directions, http://www.edu-directions.com.

HOW DO YOU CREATE AN RFP, SELECT A SHORT LIST, AND SET THE FEE?

After you've developed a list of consultant candidates, you'll write a request for proposals (RFP). This can be a fairly simple, straightforward document. Include a brief description of your school and the date when the new head will begin. Ask the firm to respond by a specified date with a proposed process, timetable, fee structure, and client list. Send the RFP to each of the firms that may be of interest.

Next, you'll select a small group of firms to interview. Typically, having a group of three or four firms will give you a good range from which to choose.

As the responses to the RFP come rolling in, you'll begin to see some distinctive characteristics in each firm. Read each proposal especially closely for tone: Does this sound like a firm that could serve your school effectively? Is it a good match with your school culture? Examine the client list for experience serving schools you consider comparable. Check reputation by contacting schools in the client list that are similar to your own, and go beyond those designated as official references if possible.

One of the distinguishing components will be fee structure. You will need to consider which formula fits your school's needs and sensibilities. Fee structure varies by firm. For example, you may find:

- Some set fees based on their sense of your size and resources.
- Others use a formula based on enrollment and operating budget.
- Still others set the fee as a percentage of the head's first-year salary. (A cautionary note: If the consultant's fee is based on the head's salary, consider managing the final compensation negotiations without the consultant's assistance to avoid any conflict of interest.)

WHAT SHOULD YOU CONSIDER WHEN INTERVIEWING SEARCH FIRM CANDIDATES?

Videoconferencing is an increasingly popular way to conduct interviews. It saves money and travel time, makes it easier to screen far-away firms, and lets you see nonverbal cues. But as handy as videoconferencing can be, you should also consider the value of an in-person interview. Meeting personally lets you see the consultant interact informally with representatives of your school and avoids the potential for distracting technology challenges.

Enter the interview process assuming that each of the search firm candidates in your select group has demonstrated competence; this will allow you to focus the consultant interviews on fit. In particular, ascertain which consultants in the firm will do the work. Often, a firm assigns a pair of consultants. In that case, try to get a feel for the dynamic between the partners and ascertain the anticipated roles of each. It could be that one is there for business development and the other will be your primary contact. You have the right to know with whom you'll be working directly.

Prepare your questions for the search firms in advance, including who in your preliminary search leadership group will take the lead on each area of inquiry. You'll find a list of suggested interview questions in Appendix C.

To orient yourself to sound ethical practices, review the NAIS Principles of Good Practice for Head Searches, including guidelines for both search committees and consultants. (See Appendix A.)

HOW DO SEARCH FIRMS—AND THE SEARCHES THEY LEAD—VARY?

In addition to using a variety of fee structures, firms differ in the number of consultants they have on board, the number of simultaneous searches they conduct, and the depth of back-office resources they have available. Some firms take care to avoid leading searches for two similar schools at the same time to reduce the possibility of candidate overlap; others appear to be less concerned about this aspect of the work. Some firms serve a wide variety of independent schools; others seem to have developed more of a niche.

Firms also differ markedly in the processes they recommend. You'll see variations in prescribed timetables; the way the firms assemble and share school profile documents; the extent to which the consultants prescreen preliminary candidates; and whether they do so on paper, by phone, by videoconference, or in person. Variations also exist at the end of the search process in the level of involvement with contract negotiations and the degree of support they provide during the transition after the appointment has been made.

As mentioned above, firms differ in their preferred search committee composition. For example, some consultants limit the search committee to trustees and then solicit broader perspectives from constituents by way of an advisory committee. If firms you're interviewing suggest this approach, inquire about their strategies for preventing a bifurcated process in which the advisory committee and search committee prefer different candidates.

Another key differentiator is the way firms consider and treat candidates. Are the ones you're reviewing known for cultivating relationships with promising school leaders? This matters because the firm you choose will represent

■ Open, Closed, and Hybrid Searches

Most searches follow a relatively transparent, or "open," process of posting the headship opening and communicating regularly to the school community as the process progresses. However, "closed" searches seem to be increasing in popularity. In such searches, prospective candidates meet with the search committee off campus, and the news of an appointment is shared only when the process is complete.

The advantage of the closed search is that it enables your school to court high-profile candidates (sitting heads in prestigious schools, for instance) without alerting the individuals' school communities that they are exploring the possibility of a move. Sometimes this approach is necessary to recruit the person who looks most desirable. Candidates who have participated in a closed-search process point to additional advantages. There is a certain freedom that comes with avoiding the school community's comparative analysis of candidates and in the opportunity to focus entirely on forging a strong, early relationship with the board during the first contacts with the school.

The open search, in contrast, offers the candidate the earliest possible opportunity to build rapport and early social/political capital with the school community. In addition, the more inclusive process offers the advantage of breadth of diverse perspectives and can serve to bind the board and school community around the shared goal of identifying the best leader for the school's future.

Some schools are experimenting with a hybrid approach that prolongs the confidential period. Search committees may be willing to try the hybrid approach to improve their chances to compete for appealing prospects. In-demand candidates may insist on it because they fear losing their jobs if word gets out that they're interviewing.

your school by name and, therefore, will spread your reputation throughout the independent school community.

Just as search firms' approaches and fees can vary, so can the work they do for you. Feel free to explore with the search firm candidates the ways they might be willing to adapt their model to suit your needs.

Throughout the process of considering search consultants, remember this:

Hybrid searches can play out in a variety of ways. A search committee may be able to protect semifinalists' confidentiality longer by traveling to them instead of having the candidates visit campus. Or the committee may replace the traditional two-interview process with three stages like these:

- **Semifinalist phase:** Interviewees meet in total confidence with only the search committee.
- **Finalist phase 1:** Selected interviewees return to speak further with the search committee, other board members, and perhaps senior staff.
- **Finalist phase 2:** Two or three remaining interviewees meet with representative groups of faculty and parents.

One school conducted an open search but took the hybrid approach for one well-qualified sitting head who was unwilling to jeopardize a job she enjoyed by openly interviewing for another. Although she did agree to meet with small groups of parents and faculty at the latest stages, she made a compelling personal case for confidentiality up to the end of the process. Her strong credentials and potential as the best person for the job proved persuasive. The search committee and board overcame their concerns about the unconventional approach and ultimately chose her.

Which approach is right for your school depends on your expectations about your candidate pool: Are there must-have candidates who might not participate in an open search? It also depends on your community's culture: Will faculty, staff, and parents trust the judgment of a small group making an important choice without broad input? The right choice requires deep self-knowledge and thoughtful consideration of the many potential ramifications for candidates, your community, and your school.

Identifying your next school leader is one of the most important responsibilities of the independent school board and can be one of the most rewarding, too.[2] This is an opportunity to affirm your school's strengths, build consensus on its needs, and develop esprit de corps throughout the school community. Your efforts to select the right consultant will set you on the path to that good work.

ENDNOTES

[1] Don Tebbe, *Chief Executive Transition: How to Hire and Support a Nonprofit CEO* (Washington, DC: BoardSource, 2008).

[2] Linda J. Shinn and Barb Nash, "A Team Approach to CEO Search," ASAE, November 7, 2014.

1. Think carefully about the sorts of guidance and expertise a search firm may be uniquely able to provide to your school.

2. Remember to focus on fit. Ask about the extent to which the consulting firm has experience with schools like yours, exhibits readiness to understand your school culture and particular needs, and offers a search process protocol that seems well-suited to your school.

3. From the initial consultant vetting process to the completion of the search, actively use counsel. Don't hesitate to ask questions so you can reap the benefit of the consultants' experience.

Choosing *Not* to Use a Search Firm

By Karla Taylor

Just as your school may want to explore alternative ways to run its search process, it may decide to consider alternatives to hiring a search consultant. Interviews with board chairs, search committee members, and experienced heads who went this route uncovered three common rationales for conducting a search without a firm.

1. **Money.** Hiring a search consultant may seem financially burdensome at a time when fees and expenses can range from $35,000 to $100,000 or even more.

2. **A unique community and culture.** Some school leaders feel that deeply knowledgeable insiders would be more effective at finding the best candidates for their school than an outside firm working off its own template.

3. **Existing expertise.** Perhaps your school has volunteers who have worked on successful searches before. Or maybe they are experienced in talent recruitment, the law, and other areas. In such cases, hiring a consultant may seem unnecessary.

Of course, going it alone means that your search committee must do all the work— or at least most of it. That makes it doubly important that committee members prepare for a major time commitment, careful planning, and close teamwork. The steps outlined in this handbook can help you understand and manage each of the key functions of the search process. The search process veterans interviewed for this sidebar also offered the following advice for schools that forgo a search consultant.

Start with strategic thinking and a candid needs assessment that engages the community.

As Chapter 1 emphasizes, it's vital to invest time in understanding your leadership needs in the context of your school's specific circumstances and within education's changing landscape. Also important, as Chapter 2 stresses, is the needs assessment, which will add to your solid foundation for both the position description and community buy-in. As part of this, make sure that the board and search committee's vision align with that of the rest of the community, including faculty, staff, and parents. One head told of a case in which poor fit between the board's dream candidate and the faculty's expectations led to a failed search and disappointment for everyone involved.

Make the most of all available resources to help you build your candidate pool, conduct your screening, and assess your candidates.

In a toolkit on its website, the Society for Human Resource Management says that even organizations with limited resources "can benefit from taking a closer look at their screening and evaluation processes to minimize hiring time and to take advantage of new technology and improved screening and evaluation techniques."[1]

The same applies to identifying and attracting candidates early in the search and assessing them at later stages.

Search tools—from networking sites like LinkedIn to HR-related tracking software—are constantly changing. If you don't have a volunteer with professional experience in up-to-date recruitment techniques, consider contracting with an HR consultant. For a fraction of the cost of a full-service independent school search consultant, you can figure out the tasks where you need the most help, whether that is developing a proactive networking strategy, screening resumes, or assessing cultural competency or leadership skills. Then outsource accordingly. Similarly, you can get legal advice from specialized law practices if your committee needs help with compliance issues. You can also contact search firms to see whether they provide certain services on an à la carte basis.

Call on the independent school network.

Advice and referrals are available through the NAIS Career Center, your state or regional associations, and colleagues at schools that are in your geographic area or are similar to yours (single sex, boarding, international, etc.). Read more about possible sources in Chapter 7.

Think about your search from the candidates' perspective.

Consultants often serve in informal but important ways to make the process smoother for applicants. One former candidate spoke of several things about a consultant-less search that left him with a bad impression of the school, whether the problem was that the search committee didn't know how to manage the process or was too overwhelmed to do so. To avoid turning off applicants:

- Have a point of contact whose job it is to answer candidate questions promptly and, if delays occur in the search process, to keep applicants informed. No applicant likes being left in the dark or having to fret about whether touching base will risk irritating the search chair.

- Provide important background materials in a timely manner—well before the finalist visit. Candidates can't accurately gauge their interest in the position without access to budgets, enrollment histories, accreditation reports, and strategic plans.

- Consider providing a resource person for candidates, someone who is not directly involved in the search but is knowledgeable about the school. This "buffer" can provide answers more dispassionately, as a consultant would. As the candidate said, "I am certain that some would feel that the search committee chair should serve in this capacity, but it is difficult to ask tough questions of the person who may have the deciding vote on your candidacy."

Recognize that good outcomes take work.

Filling a crucial position is always a challenge. For volunteers tackling the job without a consultant, it's doubly important to recognize the challenges up front.

So be patient. Be flexible. Don't waste time, but don't feel bound to an unyielding timeline. Recognize the importance of trust between and among committee members. And be honest, starting with what your school values and continuing through the ways you convey both strengths and weaknesses. That kind of authenticity is vital to finding a leader who can really help your school move forward, whether or not you're working with a search consultant.

ENDNOTE

[1] Society for Human Resource Management, Screening and Evaluating Candidates Toolkit, September 30, 2016; online at https://www.shrm.org/resourcesandtools/tools-and-samples/toolkits/pages/screeningandevaluatingcandidates.aspx.

7

Profiling the Position and Creating the Prospect Pool

By Linc Eldredge

■ Whether you're creating a description of the characteristics you seek or looking for candidates, you'll benefit from thinking broadly at first and narrowing your perspective later.

PROFILING THE POSITION

One of the most critical steps in the entire search is profiling the position. The search committee's goal is comparable to that of an architect designing the "footprint" of a foundation for a house. Houses may come in various styles, sizes, colors, and amenities, but, in all cases, the essential parameters are established when the foundation is laid.

This is not to suggest that the position description is completely unchangeable, as you can always modify it later in light of new information. Instead, the analogy is meant to emphasize the importance of constructing a picture of a person whose experience, skills, and leadership abilities align with your school's goals and objectives. You will use the position description as the base on which your entire search rests. (See Appendix D for an example.)

The position description's primary objective is to create a compelling summary of your school's culture, its goals, and the issues it faces, and to describe the characteristics of the ideal candidate for the position. This document—typically called an opportunity statement or profile—provides key information about the school and serves as a reference for prospective candidates. More important, however, a well-crafted position description will use words and phrases that, ideally, create the "aha" moment in prospective candidates—that instant that makes them want to know more about, and to be considered for, the head of school position.

Developing the position description also fulfills other objectives. The process allows your school community, working with and through your search committee, to gain a collective sense of your mission-driven institutional strategy and to visualize the characteristics of the person who will help your school achieve those goals. Communicating with the many constituents in the school community is vital. (See Chapter 4 for more about engaging the community in the head search.) Stakeholders have a wide range of institutional knowledge and wisdom to impart, and your search committee will benefit from those insights and perceptions. Equally important, the process of gathering and assimilating information gives your constituents a sense of ownership in the search and enhances transparency in a process with many confidential elements.

Put another way, following a thoughtful protocol will help make your search both more representative of the community and more credible in the eyes of the stakeholders.

Developing the Position Description

When developing a description of the characteristics you're seeking in the new head of school, you need to step back and look at the broader picture. Accordingly, there are five major points to address when you are creating the profile:

1. What is the history of your school, and how has it shaped the present culture and the way its mission is articulated?
2. What does your school wish to become with the guidance of this new leadership?
3. What issues, challenges, and opportunities will this individual face?
4. What technical knowledge and skills are necessary for the person's success?
5. What leadership style and personal characteristics are likely to fit best with your school and thereby make the new head successful in your culture?

Although you might be tempted to go immediately to Points 4 and 5 when beginning to discuss the ideal school head, it is better to start by addressing Points 1, 2, and 3. Why?

First of all, the school is hiring for the future. You're seeking someone who will transform the school, whether dramatically or incrementally. Having a solid working hypothesis about what the future should look like is necessary to inform your decision-making.

Second, prospective candidates will want to understand clearly the challenges and opportunities they will encounter at your school. Some people will self-select out of the search; others will be intrigued or invigorated by the description and seek to be included in the candidate pool.

Only after your school has determined its broad strategic direction and defined the issues it faces should your search committee determine the skills, knowledge, personal characteristics, and leadership style that the new head should bring. If you have adequately assessed your school's needs following the steps outlined in Chapter 2, you will be able to clearly articulate these priorities and move forward. One way to visualize this concept is as an inverted pyramid:

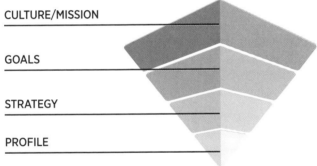

CULTURE/MISSION

GOALS

STRATEGY

PROFILE

Source: Brigham Hill Consultancy

Simply put, you must first grasp the culture and mission of your school, understand its long-term institutional goals, and articulate its strategic direction. Only then can you accurately describe the traits of the new head of school and ensure that those traits align with your organization's needs.

Formatting the Position Description

How do you construct the position description so that it will be both informative and compelling enough to stimulate the "aha" response? Consider organizing it in the following way.

Part 1: A description of the school

- *Provide a brief history* going back to the school's founding and the values on which it was launched. You may want to share key events or anecdotes from the school's history that help define its present ethos. Such an overview gives a sense of vitality to your institution and, perhaps more important, provides context for the next section, in which you ...

- *Outline the school's current status.* This typically includes facts and figures regarding enrollment, finances, endowment, physical plant, academic achievement, unique programs, and similar concrete elements that help the prospective candidate get a sense of perspective about the opportunity.

- *Explain the school's aspirations for the future.* What academic goals and other outcomes does your school seek for its graduates? What constituencies will you serve? How might the school community itself change over time? Will the school experience be different five years from now and, if so, in what ways? Will the institution change in terms of enrollment, physical size, finances, curriculum, or programs? Although the school's core values will probably not change, will you express them in different ways?

Articulating the school's values and aspirations gives a contour to the head's role and will help attract prospective candidates whose personal values and aspirations are aligned with those of the school.

Part 2: Key responsibilities of the new head of school

Although virtually every head of school job description contains the same elements, certain duties will be more important than others for executing your school's current strategy. Those components should get special emphasis. Typically, they would come first in a series of bulleted points in the job description, beginning with the most critical and descending to the less vital elements.

Part 3: Credentials—the experience base, skills, and knowledge necessary to carry out the school's strategy

This section usually includes the following:

- Academic credentials

- Years of experience
- Background by institution type (with information about size, pedagogy, day or boarding, geographic, and other considerations)
- Experience in managing people, programs, budgets, and fundraising
- Knowledge of educational theory and practice
- Ability to communicate with constituents
- Experience in building and sustaining inclusive learning communities
- Background in facilities development
- Proficiency in applying technology
- Experience with innovating and developing new programs

Part 4: Leadership—personal characteristics of the ideal head of school
Who is the human being behind the credentials? Bearing in mind that leaders are those who create followers, ask these questions: What are the traits and stylistic elements of the person who will inspire your school community and therefore help transform it according to its institutional strategy? How would you describe this person's value system, sense of calling, ability to serve as a role model, decision-making approach, interpersonal and leadership style, and other intangible elements that will motivate the school's stakeholders?

IDENTIFYING AND RECRUITING CANDIDATES

A head search usually benefits from creating a large and diverse pool of prospective candidates, which you later winnow to a smaller number in light of the position description and your evaluation of the relative merits of each candidate. A broad pool benefits the search committee for several reasons:

- *It's educational*, especially for a group of volunteers who do not normally evaluate prospects for a headship. Seeing a range of possibilities is helpful both for getting the lay of the land and for creating various scenarios of how prospects could lead in your school's environment. Think of this process as testing the hypothesis posed by the position description and then using your prospect review to refine your collective thinking, particularly regarding the relationship between credentials and leadership.

- *It helps the search committee keep an open mind.* Think back to the house foundation analogy at the beginning of this chapter. Just as several types

Legal Considerations of Candidate Screening

By Debra P. Wilson

When your search committee begins the candidate screening process, keep in mind these two areas of concern.

1. **Confidentiality.** Many individuals who are searching for head positions have not disclosed this interest to their current employers and may choose not to do so until later in the process. Your search committee members should take all necessary steps to ensure that they do not violate confidentiality at any time in the search process.

2. **Bias.** Your job description, and the requirements that go with it, must not be used to weed out candidates on the basis of any protected category, including age, race, ethnicity, or religion (unless the school is a religious entity). Similarly, you may not sort applications by protected classes, even if you're doing it to ensure that minority applicants are in the final round.

This issue presents your search committee with challenges from two sides. On the one hand, like many schools, yours may be seeking to diversify its staff. On the other, legally you may not consider race or gender within your hiring process.

That said, you can ensure that you post job openings in places where minority and other candidates may be more likely to seek job openings. You can also conduct an initial "blind" review of resumes and applications to ensure that implicit bias does not play into your committee's decisions. Read more about this in Chapters 9 and 10.

---

of houses can be designed to fit a particular foundation, the baseline that your position description provides can accommodate candidates of different styles and backgrounds. Thus, you may have a pool of individuals under consideration who both fit the broader parameters of the sort of person you seek and also represent a variety of personality types and experiences.

- *It expands your available choices.* The market for highly accomplished leaders is very competitive. No matter how attractive you think your school is, other institutions may be more appealing to your favorite candidate, and for that reason you may not be able to hire your first or second choice. It's important to have qualified backup candidates you can revisit.

- *It may contain a pleasant surprise.* Every now and then, a candidate who initially appears less attractive is later found to be a perfect match for the position. By generating a broad pool during the early stages, you remain open to such a happy circumstance.

Finding Candidates

Your position description is in place, and your search committee is in agreement about the value of seeking out a broad pool of candidates. How do you find the best prospects for your search?

In two ways: active and passive. Most successful searches combine both techniques to create the broad pool you seek. This is an area in which search consultants are most helpful, since they have access to a broad network they have likely developed over a period of years and they possess knowledge of the profession's leadership and outreach networks. If your school is undertaking the search independently, this may be your most challenging task. But whether your school is working on its own or in tandem with a consultant, it is helpful to understand the following approaches.

1. **Passive sourcing** involves advertising your opportunity in venues that prospective candidates might see. There are two general categories.
   - *Print and online advertising.* Your ad can get broad exposure through publications such as the *The Blue Sheet* (published by Educational Directions, Inc.), the *Chronicle of Higher Education, Education Week,* and the *New York Times,* as well as NAIS's online Career Center. In addition, several regional independent school associations and organizations have digital and print career resources.
   - *Specialty advertising.* Examples of this category include print and online media for specific fields such as learning differences, schools with religious affiliations, single-sex institutions, traditionally underrepresented groups, Montessori schools, International Baccalaureate or gifted programs, and early childhood education.

2. **Active sourcing** involves contacting prospective candidates or those

who might be able to refer such people to you. This approach assumes that your ideal candidate may not currently be contemplating a career move. Even if a person is generally aware of your search, the opening may not have seemed initially to be of interest. Accordingly, a proactive approach allows you to access a hidden market of possible candidates by expanding the pool of prospects beyond those individuals who apply directly. It also broadens your access to a diverse candidate pool. In addition to employing professional networking sites such as LinkedIn, other techniques you can use include these:

- *Direct personal calls.* This method is the best because it involves person-to-person discussions. When properly approached, a "source" (such as a head of school) can be engaged in conversation in hopes that the discussion will stimulate thoughts about networking and lead to a referral—or, perhaps, motivate that person to explore the opportunity personally.

- *Volume mailings.* This approach involves eliciting recommendations by sending an email or letter with the job description to school heads and other knowledgeable people. To make your effort effective, you should both personalize it and strategically target it to people in certain types of schools. The message should articulate clearly and succinctly why you're seeking the recipient's input and highlight the two or three key points within the job description that you hope will spur the person's thought process and lead to a referral.

Again, this approach is most successful when you target people who are active in networks that include possible candidates who fit your profile. For example, your incumbent head of school may know such people, and using the head's name will provide you with ready access and credibility. One source call can lead to referrals to other knowledgeable sources, whom you can then contact and ask about yet further referrals. Over time, this method helps the search committee create a web of contacts who will both support your continuing education and expose you to a large number of qualified people.

If you also make cold calls, try to identify school heads who you believe would know the sort of person you seek by virtue of geography, mission, and size of school; pedagogy; religious affiliation; learning specialty; single-sex education; or whatever other parameters apply. Most sources will not mind being contacted if they believe your call is based on a specific affiliation and not part of an untargeted mass-calling program.

Building a Diverse Candidate Pool

As noted earlier, your school will benefit from a large and varied candidate pool in the early stages. Increasingly, independent schools are committed to cultivating equity and inclusion in their communities and to broadening their student, faculty, staff, and family populations with people of diverse backgrounds. Accordingly, schools often seek to develop head of school candidate pools that represent diversity of race, ethnicity, religion, national origin, sex, gender identity, sexual orientation, and other characteristics.

Many groups, such as people of color and women, are historically underrepresented among heads of school and other senior administrators. Therefore, creating a diverse candidate pool typically requires a proactive approach to sourcing and identifying prospective candidates.

One good source of information and support is NAIS, which has put considerable emphasis on diversity. You will undoubtedly want to learn more about NAIS's resources. For more on building and working with a diverse pool, also see the chapters in the next section of this book.

Traditional and Nontraditional Candidates

The concept of a varied candidate pool also covers candidates from nontraditional professional backgrounds—that is, people with experience in organizations other than independent schools.[*] Frankly, most searches focus exclusively on traditional candidates—heads or other senior administrators of independent schools, including internal candidates currently employed by your school. Although this seems more efficient because you can target both your active and your passive sourcing, restricting your search this way might mean that you miss the best match for your school.

It may be wise to be especially open to nontraditional candidates during the early stages of your search, both to identify strong leaders in fields not normally

---

[*] In recent years, the terms "traditional" and "nontraditional" have become ambiguous when applied to head candidates. Many people use—or hear—the terms as euphemisms for "white males" (traditional) and "candidates who are women or people of color" (nontraditional). For the purposes of this section, the term "traditional" applies only to professional background—those people emerging from the independent school ranks as opposed to corporate, higher education, or other nonprofit roles.

scoured for school heads and to provide contrast and definition to search committee members as they continue their education about whom they are seeking.

So where do you find candidates who may possess the skills, knowledge, experience, and leadership attributes you seek but who gained those skills in a non-independent school environment?

There is no one answer. Where you look depends on your school and its particular institutional strategy. If your committee deems such candidates important and you're working with a search firm, it is essential to let your consultant know this at the outset.

Defining such universes requires a good deal of creativity and unconventional thinking—not to mention serendipity. In effect, you hope that while you're investigating a non-independent school field, you'll be lucky enough either to find a prospective candidate who is intrigued by your opportunity or to be talking with a source who has an enlightened idea at the moment when you make contact.

With those provisos, here are several fields you may wish to consider as you launch your creative thought process.

- **Nonacademic independent school administrators.** If your school is having financial difficulty, you may find your successful candidate among the many highly accomplished business officers or CFOs serving independent schools. Likewise, if fundraising ability is key, you might consider directors of development or advancement with strong general management skills.

- **Public school superintendents.** Many high-quality public school districts have student bodies that are demographically comparable to independent schools and parent bodies with high academic aspirations and expectations. If your school is large and complex or if you are among the relatively few independent schools with a faculty union, district superintendents may be good prospects.

- **College administrators.** Academic leaders such as deans or provosts in higher education—as well as presidents of small liberal arts colleges—can often make a successful move to the independent school world. They can be good prospects if your school is relatively large and you have an upper school division with a strong college prep and college counseling program. Bear in mind, however, that higher education tends to be more structured and administratively more formal than independent schools. So if you're considering someone from a college, it is particularly important to match the candidate's personality to your school culture.

- **Museum and other "educational campus" directors.** Many science, natural history, art, and specialty museums as well as zoos, botanical gardens, and aquariums share several characteristics with independent schools. They have high intellectual content and are dedicated to teaching and education. Curators may once have been faculty and often possess similar interests and personality types. The physical plant is typically a campus with technology, security, dining, and maintenance issues comparable to those of a school. And their top administrators work with engaged boards of trustees, spend time fundraising, and are essentially chief executive officers of complex businesses. Thus, some schools may find this background attractive.

- **Retired senior government officials or military officers.** Though this may seem like an unlikely universe in which to find candidates, depending on your needs, it can be fruitful. For example, a military school might seek a retired military officer with a strong educational foundation and a desire for a second career. Likewise, Foreign Service officers typically can retire in their early 50s, when they are at their intellectual and professional peak. Such individuals presumably have proven leadership abilities, interact frequently with think tanks and otherwise deal with intellectual content, are persuasive and diplomatic with a variety of demanding constituencies, are usually adept at crisis management, and bring a worldly perspective.

- **Executives of private foundations or nongovernmental organizations (NGOs).** Many such private organizations are oriented toward research or advocacy in the sciences, social sciences, and humanities. Moreover, their executives frequently have advanced academic degrees and move comfortably among scholars and educators.

- **People working in an independent school as a second career** whose earlier experience in the business world or similar environment allows them to bring chief executive officer acumen to the complexity of a modern independent school.

As you determine whether to look in nontraditional fields, consider this advice.

- **Be creative!** Brainstorm as a search committee about your specific needs and try to imagine what a nontraditional candidate might look like. No idea is too outlandish, at least at the beginning, and sometimes the most unlikely suggestion will spur yet more creative thinking and help you identify qualified candidates.

- **Discuss the issue of nontraditional candidates frequently to keep the topic at the front of your committee members' minds.** Remember the importance of serendipity. You want to be able to recognize and exploit good fortune when it comes your way; your luck will improve if all of you are constantly scanning the horizon.

- **Don't be surprised if your pool of nontraditional candidates is thin.** Such people are hard to define, let alone to find, and even then they may be difficult to interest in the prospect of a career change.

- **Don't feel that the exercise has been a failure if you ultimately select a traditional candidate.** Apart from being in good company, you will have benefited from the mind stretching that comes with a search for nontraditional individuals. The education you gain will make your final decision that much better.

THE IMPORTANT ROLES OF HARD WORK AND GOOD LUCK

The following chapters go into greater depth about bias and its impact on your search—both important considerations that will inform the process of profiling your position and recruiting candidates. But by this point, you can clearly see that a successful search is a combination of working smart, working hard, and exploiting good fortune when you find it. The old adage is forever true: Luck is when preparation and opportunity meet. If you persevere, use your intelligence and instincts, and take advantage of serendipity when it comes your way, your search for a strong prospective candidate pool will ultimately be successful.

1. Be inclusive as you develop the position description so you can make it representative of your school community and credible to stakeholders.

2. Develop a well-organized position description that offers history, program summary, key responsibilities of the new head, expected credentials, and desired personal characteristics.

3. Use multiple avenues to promote the position, such as print and online advertising, specialty advertising, professional networking sites, direct personal contact, and volume mailings.

4. Understand the importance of a diverse candidate pool.

5. Decide whether you want to deliberately consider applicants from non-school professional backgrounds.

Keep an open mind. Don't fill the ideal candidate profile with a string of requirements that rule out good people. For example, automatically requiring a Ph.D. needlessly eliminates 99 percent of the world. Requiring experience as a head of school rules out rising stars who are more than ready to take on a first headship. Many of the best placements I have made are these rising stars.

John Magagna, Founding Director, Search Associates

Don't look for "God on a good day." In your position statement, prioritize three to five leadership qualities (such as educational leadership, fundraising, personnel management, or financial planning) instead of producing a document that describes a person supremely well-qualified in all areas. Building consensus among faculty, staff, trustees, and parents around those priorities will make the rest of the search go more smoothly, especially at the finalist stage.

Lee Quinby, Executive Director, Association of Colorado Independent Schools

Beware of profiling pitfalls. (1) Avoid the "pendulum swing," unintentionally hiring an individual who is the polar opposite of the predecessor. The longer a previous head has been in place, the more likely this is to occur, and the abrupt change can be a shock to the school's system. (2) Don't adhere so rigidly to your profile that you fail to even consider an out-of-the-box candidate who could be an excellent choice.

John Littleford, Senior Partner, Littleford & Associates

8

What Research Tells Us About Improving Diversity in the Talent Pool

By Amada Torres and Caroline G. Blackwell

▓ NAIS research indicates that relatively few people of color and white women have advanced to headships. But the studies also point to specific opportunities for improvement.

Research highlights the connection between diversity and overall performance in the business world. A McKinsey study called "Why Diversity Matters" found that companies in the top quartile for racial and ethnic diversity were 35 percent more likely to have financial returns above their industry medians. Similarly, companies in the top quartile for gender diversity were 15 percent more likely to outperform their peers.[1]

But diversity improves more than the bottom line. It enhances creativity and leads teams to breakthrough innovations, as reported by Katherine W. Phillips in her article "How Diversity Makes Us Smarter." This is not only because people with different backgrounds bring new information. Interacting with groups of diverse colleagues also prepares individuals to be more open to alternative viewpoints and to reach consensus.[2]

Increasingly, independent school search committees recognize the benefits of hiring people of color and white women in headship positions. Racially, ethnically, and culturally diverse leaders are known to do many things: inspire students, attract more diverse staff, broaden a school's perspective about education and its reach into new markets, and create a vision that connects the school's mission with the opportunities presented by the changing educational landscape. Beyond advancing diversity for its business value, such leaders are also committed to diversity and inclusion as the right thing to do.[3]

Despite these benefits, progress has been slow. Among NAIS member schools surveyed in 2013, 96 percent of board chairs and 96 percent of heads of school were white.[4] These statistics are comparable to those in the wider nonprofit sector, in which a 2017 BoardSource study found that 90 percent of CEOs and 90 percent of board chairs were white.[5] The lack of racial, ethnic, and cultural diversity at the highest levels of institutional leadership, and among executive recruiters, poses a structural impediment to advancement throughout the nonprofit sector, according to *Race to Lead*, a pioneering 2017 study on the industry's racial leadership gap.[6]

This chapter addresses what NAIS research indicates about ethnic, racial, and gender diversity and the headship. It also covers ways independent school leaders and the search committees they construct can take action to broaden their candidate pools and mitigate bias in the overall hiring process.

WHAT THE DATA SHOW

In 2017-2018, only 36 percent of NAIS school heads were women and 7 percent were people of color, according to NAIS research (Figure 1). Between 2000-2001 and 2017-2018, slight progress occurred in the number of heads of color in NAIS schools. But the numbers for female heads remained about the same.

This lack of representation matters because having diverse leaders is more important than ever, given research that demonstrates that a racially and ethnically diverse faculty and administration have academic and social benefits for all students.[7] Furthermore, diverse leadership mirrors the changing demographics of the school-age population in the United States. According to the U.S. Department of Education, in 2014 there were more students of color than white students in public K-12 schools.[8] This milestone was achieved mainly because of the dramatic growth in the Hispanic population and the decline in the non-Hispanic white population, but also because of a steady rise in the number of Asian-Americans. (The number of African-Americans has remained mostly flat.)

These same demographic trends are reflected in NAIS schools. The number of students of color increased from 21.0 percent in 2005-2006 to 29.3 percent in 2017-2018 (Figure 2).[9] This shift is likely to continue. Projections from

Figure 1: Female Heads and Heads of Color at NAIS Schools

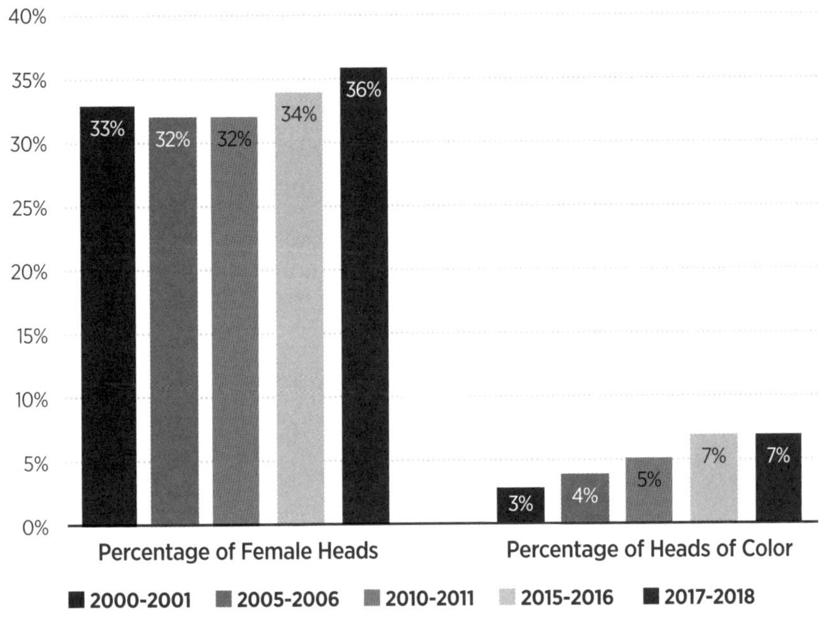

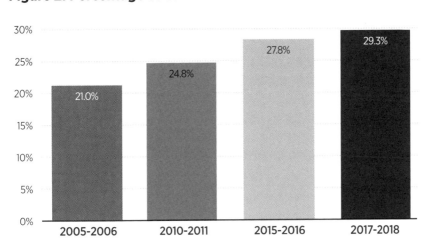

Source: NAIS, Percentage of Female Heads and Heads of Color, Data and Analysis for School Leadership (DASL)

Figure 2: Percentage of Students of Color in NAIS Schools

Source: NAIS, Students of Color as a Percentage of Total Enrollment, DASL

Figure 3: Percentage of U.S. Children Ages 0-17 by Race and Ethnicity, Selected Years and Projections

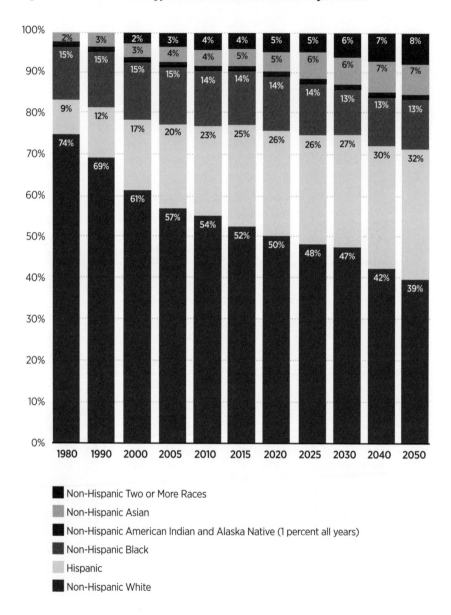

Non-Hispanic Two or More Races
Non-Hispanic Asian
Non-Hispanic American Indian and Alaska Native (1 percent all years)
Non-Hispanic Black
Hispanic
Non-Hispanic White

Source: U.S. Census Bureau, Population

the U.S. Census Bureau indicate that, after 2020, less than half of the children in the United States will be non-Hispanic white (Figure 3).

UNDERSTANDING SEARCH PHASES AND THEIR PITFALLS

To explore the recruitment dynamics that contribute to or hinder the hiring of people of color and white women, in 2016 NAIS conducted a qualitative study that included in-depth interviews with search firms and search committee chairs. The interviews revealed a layered search process with five different phases: discovery, candidate recruitment, pool narrowing, interviews, and final decision (Figure 4). Understanding these phases, as well as other search-related insights the NAIS study uncovered, helps you see that there are many opportunities to improve the process and diversify the candidate pool. (A list of action steps schools can take throughout this process appears at the end of this section of the book. These steps highlight ways to increase the diversity of candidate pools and avoid pitfalls in all phases of the search process.)

Figure 4: The Five Phases of the Head Search Process

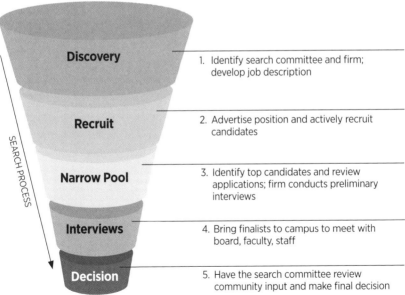

Source: NAIS Study on Hiring Practices

Discovery

During the discovery phase, schools in the NAIS study assembled their search committees. All the committees included board members, and many were made up of faculty, parents, and community members as well. At this point, most but not all schools also hired a search firm or consultant to guide them through the hiring process. Schools that had existing relationships with particular search firms or consultants often turned to them without interviewing other options. When hiring a new search firm, the search committees or boards interviewed three to five firms before making a decision.

To lay a foundation during the discovery phase for a more diverse pool, your school can take these steps:

- Make racial, ethnic, and cultural diversity a strategic institutional priority for hiring at all professional levels.
- Enlist individuals with different demographic and cultural backgrounds to serve on your search committee.
- Carefully review candidate requirements and the way experience will be evaluated.
- Before hiring a search firm, interview its consultants about their methods, resources, and track record in recruiting people of color and white women for leadership positions in independent schools.

Recruitment

NAIS conducted a qualitative study of the recruitment phase. Among schools that hired consultants, the search firms were typically in charge of the process at this point. When promoting positions, consultants primarily relied on outreach to their networks. They also kept databases of candidates and reached out to current heads and administrators to see whether they were looking for a change. Some search committees referred internal candidates to their firm or asked the firm to reach out to contacts who might make strong candidates.

Although some search firms developed a recruitment pool of white women and people of color, others placed less emphasis on this approach. If your committee determines that your pool does not have enough people of color and white women, go back to the search firm and ask for a more culturally diverse candidate pool. Whether or not you are working with a firm, your committee should also conduct proactive outreach to people of color and white women.

Pool Narrowing

At this stage, search firms reported having different methods and criteria for selecting which candidates to present to the search committee. Firms generally presented between 10 and 30 candidates. The firms reported trying to include people of color and white women at this point, especially if the search committee had explicitly asked that this be done.

The factors that search firms said helped candidates stand out to them during the pool-narrowing phase included the quality of their written applications, their fit with school culture, their experience at similar schools and schools with similar focus areas, their proven record, and their fit with the geographic region.

Since search firms use their own judgment and criteria to decide whom to present, their own implicit biases may put certain candidates at a disadvantage. That's why your search committee needs to be proactive in taking these steps:

- Lead the search process by participating in anti-bias training (implicit and explicit) so that your school can establish a process that is fair and appropriate for all candidates.
- Discuss and determine the criteria the search firm will use to select which applicants to share.
- Set clear expectations and guidelines about the types of candidates the school wants to see, including diversity requirements.
- State that you want the search firm to keep an open mind about candidates with experience that may be unfamiliar.

These steps are equally important for schools that are not using a search firm.

Interviews

At this stage, it is easy to measure the breadth of diversity in head searches. The NAIS study found that most schools had white women at the finalist stage, but many did not have people of color. As the next two chapters make clear, search committees need to be mindful of the role that implicit or explicit bias may play during the interviews and the selection of candidates at this point.

Decision

At this all-important stage after the finalist visits, the NAIS study found the following:

- Search firms or committees gathered feedback from the school community through surveys and interview evaluations.
- When making their final choice, search committees observed the candidates' interactions with the school community and the school community's reaction to the candidates.
- Most search committees aimed for a consensus choice among committee members.
- The final decision often came down to personality and perceived fit with the school.

Throughout the five stages, it's clear that search committees will maintain a diverse pool only if they have a clearly delineated and continuously evaluated search process, coupled with demonstrable, unambiguous selection criteria. Your committee needs to be particularly conscious of ways in which personal and institutional biases may affect perceptions of candidates and the impact these prejudices may have on the final choice.

OBSTACLES TO DIVERSIFYING THE POOL

NAIS research uncovered two common factors that make it harder to maintain a broad pool of candidates for consideration.

1. Seeking headship experience

In interviews, search committees and search firms both reported having a long list of requirements of the kind that, in most cases, only a head of school would possess. Since people of color and white women are already underrepresented in headship positions, this approach presents both a practical and a structural obstacle. It also limits opportunity for those who hold nonacademic leadership roles within schools.

The 2017-2018 NAIS statistics (Table 1) show that the highest representation of female leaders occurs in the roles of lower school head and admissions and development directors. The largest number of independent school leaders of color are concentrated in diversity director roles. Placing a premium on experience that only individuals at the highest reaches would have, and using that marker to rule out candidates, can heighten disadvantage for people of color and white women. This is particularly true when position descriptions and decision-making processes fail to specify or assess behavioral criteria that would allow all candidates to demonstrate comparable, applicable work experience.

Table 1: Percentages of Female and People of Color Leaders in Selected Roles, 2017-2018

Position	Females	People of Color
Business Officer	55%	11%
Associate Head	51%	7%
Assistant Head	63%	15%
Upper School Head	39%	8%
Middle School Head	55%	13%
Lower School Head	85%	11%
Director of Development	79%	9%
Director of Admissions	77%	14%
Director of Diversity	68%	95%

Source: NAIS, Staff by Gender, DASL

2. Relying on superficial characteristics to determine "cultural fit"

Analysis of the search process also revealed that search committees and firms strongly emphasized the notion of candidates' cultural fit with their school. Independent schools are not unlike employers worldwide who prioritize a candidate's ability to reflect, adapt to, and uphold core institutional values and beliefs. Seeking a high degree of compatibility is both a ubiquitous goal and a subjective measurement.

Because of the subjectivity inherent in assessing cultural fit, schools can risk replicating patterns of bias that have long shut out people of color and white women. This is true when surface characteristics such as race and gender are tagged as "nontraditional." It's also true when objective, job-specific qualifications are ignored in favor of a shared racial or cultural background or a common alma mater. Selecting candidates on the basis of whether the committee likes spending time with them in social situations[10] can also reinforce a disturbing perception: that independent schools have trouble seeing people of color and white women as capable of sharing and upholding core values that are essential to educational excellence, community development, and the like.

Throughout the chapters in this section, you'll read about how search committees and consultants can remove obstacles and increase the objectivity and rigor of their search process for all candidates. For example, one now-classic strategy is the redacted, or "blind," screening process. It prevents evaluators from seeing or knowing the racial, ethnic, or gender identity of a candidate. This approach has proven to increase the probability that people of color and white women will advance in the hiring process.[11]

In an educational landscape where exceptional leadership can make the difference between a thriving teaching and learning community and an institution in peril, your independent school has a golden opportunity. You can cultivate an authentically diverse and inclusive community that is a beacon for exceptional talent and reflects the range of diversity our constituencies comprise. You can also employ culturally competent hiring strategies and practices to recruit a fresh class of heads of schools who will help the industry make a new mark on American education.

ENDNOTES

[1] Vivian Hunt, Dennis Layton, and Sara Prince, "Why Diversity Matters," McKinsey Insights, January 2015; online at https://www.mckinsey.com/business-functions/organization/our-insights/why-diversity-matters.

[2] Katherine W. Phillips, "How Diversity Makes Us Smarter," *Scientific American,* September 16, 2014; online at http://www.pcusa.org/site_media/media/uploads/vocation/pdf/how_diversity_makes_us_smarter_scientificamerican_sept_16_2014.pdf.

[3] Amy Stuart Wells, Lauren Fox, and Diana Cordova-Cobo, *How Racially Diverse Schools and Classrooms Can Benefit All Students* (New York: Century Foundation, 2016); online at https://s3-us-west-2.amazonaws.com/production.tcf.org/app/uploads/2016/02/09142501/HowRaciallyDiverse_AmyStuartWells-11.pdf.

[4] National Association of Independent Schools (NAIS), *Heads and Boards Working in Partnership: 2012-13 NAIS Governance Study* (Washington, DC: NAIS, 2013).

[5] BoardSource, *Leading With Intent: 2017 National Index of Nonprofit Board Practices* (Washington, DC: BoardSource, 2017); online at https://leadingwithintent.org/wp-content/uploads/2017/11/LWI-2017.pdf?utm_referrer=https%3A%2F%2Fleadingwithintent.org%2F.

[6] Sean Thomas-Breitfeld and Frances Kunreuther, *Race to Lead: Confronting the Nonprofit Racial Leadership Gap* (New York: Building Movement Project, 2017); online at http://www.buildingmovement.org/pdf/RacetoLead_NonprofitRacialLeadershipGap.pdf.

[7] Wells et al., *How Racially Diverse Schools and Classrooms Can Benefit All Students.*

[8] U.S. Department of Education, National Center for Education Statistics, "Table 203.50: Enrollment and percentage distribution of enrollment in public elementary and secondary

schools, by race/ethnicity and region: Selected years, fall 1995 through fall 2023," *Digest of Education Statistics*; online at http://nces.ed.gov/programs/digest/d13/tables/dt13_203.50.asp.

[9] NAIS Data and Analysis for School Leadership (DASL), Table 400: Students of Color as a Percentage of Total Enrollment, 5 Years: Industry 2005-06, 2010-11, and 2015-16.

[10] Peter Swanson, "Managers, the Beer Test Is the Wrong Way to Hire," *PayScale: Career News*, May 31, 2016; online at http://www.payscale.com/career-news/2016/03/managers-the-beer-test-is-the-wrong-way-to-hire.

[11] Claudia Goldin and Cecilia Rouse, "Orchestrating Impartiality: The Impact of 'Blind' Auditions on Female Musicians," *American Economic Review*, September 2000; online at http://pubs.aeaweb.org/doi/pdfplus/10.1257/aer.90.4.715.

1. Understand how and why underrepresentation of people of color and white women is a major problem in a time of rapidly changing demographics.

2. Recognize that heads of schools and trustees have the responsibility and the power to eliminate institutional barriers that contribute to the racial and gender leadership gaps in independent schools.

3. Be aware of the five typical hiring phases and how your search committee (and your search firm, if you have one) can make them more culturally responsive and inclusive.

4. Recognize that independent schools are unlikely to increase the number of heads who are people of color or white women if they eliminate people without headship experience from the candidate pool.

5. Don't be fooled by an unexamined notion of cultural fit.

Make your goals clear. Diversity isn't a nice-to-have but a must-have. If the expectation is that the search firm will present a pool that more closely represents the makeup that the school aspires to, the conversation is better and more robust.

Pete Gillin, Managing Director, Diversified Search

Avoid shrinking the pool of potential candidates too quickly. Make sure you don't overlook talented individuals, especially educators of color and women, who might lack past headship experience but demonstrate a willingness to learn and possess other attributes that would enable them to be very successful.

Chris Fleischner, President, CalWest Educators Placement

Beware the "good fit" trap. Often search committees lack diversity, and they most often recommend to the board a candidate who "seems like a good fit." This can translate—unconsciously, most likely—to "this person looks like us" or "like past heads we've known."

Claudia Daggett, Executive Director, Independent Schools Association of the Central States (ISACS)

9

Types of Bias in the Search Process

By Doreen S. Oleson and Thomas P. Olverson

■ An important way to improve the search process is to understand the bias that search committee members bring to the table and then work to mitigate it.

In his book *Thinking, Fast and Slow*, Nobel Prize-winner Daniel Kahneman details the prejudice that runs rampant in human decision-making and highlights the illusion of objectivity that pervades human thinking. A summary of research that he and other psychologists conducted since the 1980s, the book provides a conceptual framework for exploring the prejudices that infect any group's collective judgment.[1]

This flawed decision-making is evident in the work of independent school search committees tasked with selecting new heads of school. In fact, the bias is so palpable that Kahneman's book should be required reading for all members of a newly formed search committee.

This chapter will touch on common types of bias and important ways to overcome them.

THREE TYPES OF BIAS

1. The Priming Bias

The priming bias is sometimes referred to as "deficit hiring bias." In a school setting, this particular type of irrational thinking involves identifying the attributes of the present head of school and assigning them unwarranted weight in the selection of the next head.

For instance, if a head is perceived as having weak relationships with students, the search committee may decide, almost without thinking, that it is imperative that the next head be someone who will develop great relationships with students. It may be helpful for the next head to have this attribute. But too often, search committee members unwisely elevate its importance, and their perceptions of the current head prime the unconscious value placed on student relationships.

2. The Halo Bias

Let's say a candidate comes from a highly regarded school that search committee members admire. Their perception of the prestigious school may become a powerful proxy for all the candidate's attributes. In turn, this perception leads to hiring committee thinking that goes something like this:

- This candidate comes from a prestigious school.
- We wish our school were more like the candidate's school.
- We should hire this candidate.

Many of us "rational" folk might scoff at the simplicity of this thinking. But the same reasoning is the foundation of the many advertisements that sell cars, soft drinks, and myriad other consumer goods with great success.

3. The Beauty Contest Bias

Kahneman refers to this as the "availability heuristic."[2] Absent the hard work, discipline, and rigor it takes to amass evidence that a candidate possesses the attributes the search committee has identified as critical, search committee members instead ask themselves the easy question, "Do we like this candidate?"

A strong search committee consists of representatives from multiple constituencies. Committee members may hire a consultant or recruit capable volunteer leaders to guide them through the process. They champion transparency. But these key initial steps may provide false comfort—and the illusion that objectivity rules the day. This is often not the case.

A given candidate may knock it out of the park in an interview by demonstrating that she really "gets" the school. But, in essence, she is simply validating the committee members' love of the school. In some cases, her enthusiasm for the school and her desire to land the job draw committee members to her. Post-interview, they then look for evidence to support their initial emotional connection with the candidate (an example of what's called "confirmation bias"). They fail to go back to the attributes of the ideal leader and ask the question, "What evidence in the candidate's writing, interviews, and recommendations demonstrates that she has the requisite skills, experience, personality, and knowledge to be the leader our school needs going forward?"

To answer that question requires hard work. Unfortunately, as Kahneman so convincingly reveals, we humans would rather go with the easy, intuitive answer than one that is supported by evidence.

OVERCOMING HIRING BIAS

At the end of this section of the *Head Search Handbook* are action steps to help with the hard work of getting beyond the easy solution. But here are details about techniques we have found especially helpful for neutralizing the impact of bias.

Make Time for Probing Interviews

One powerful tool is the extended interview. It's a detailed conversation designed to reveal candidates' leadership skills by talking about their past behavior when they faced a range of challenges. This kind of interview can help establish a robust narrative about the candidate that will be reinforced or modified as your committee gathers evidence from subsequent interviews, meetings with constituents, and reference checking.

One of the most illuminating interviews we ever conducted was with a head of an elementary school in a mid-size city in the Northeast. Focusing on past experience, we asked her about the biggest communication challenge she faced since becoming a head. For the next 20 minutes, we delved into a problem she had with a veteran teacher. We peppered her with questions as she told the story. In the process, we began to learn about her leadership strengths. She believed in collaboration and a willingness to hold teachers accountable for demonstrating it. She insisted that teachers contribute to the school's growth by bringing their imaginations and initiative to the table every day. And she admitted that she had yet to solve the problem but was determined to do so.

Soon we knew why this head had, in four short years, increased enrollment by almost 50 percent in a city where Catholic schools dominated and families were hardly aware of independent school education. She was a true leader, not content with mere action but focused on results.

Riffing on a Ralph Waldo Emerson quote, former National Football League

■ To Diminish Bias, Diversify Your Search Committee

A key component in mitigating bias is a diverse search committee. The evidence is overwhelming. According to Lisa Burrell in her article "We Just Can't Handle Diversity," decades of studies show that "a diverse workforce measurably improves decision-making, problem-solving, creativity, innovation, and flexibility."[3]

The same principle can be applied to a search committee. Having multiple perspectives—often but not exclusively born from an ethnically and socioeconomically diverse membership that transcends mere representation from various school constituencies—increases the chances that the school will make a better choice. As Burrell persuasively argues, people delude themselves into thinking that they can readily and objectively identify talent: "We believe we know good talent when we see it, yet we usually don't—we're terrible at evaluating people objectively."[4]

Piggybacking on this argument, Lauren Rivera's book *Pedigree* delves into the unconscious bias that defines decision-making by like-minded, albeit overconfident, hiring committees. Rivera studied "hiring processes in some of the nation's highest-paying entry-level jobs." For candidates in the middle of the pack of candidates, smooth communication skills, or "polish," became the critical criteria for moving an application to

coach Chuck Knox once said, "Nothing speaks so loudly as your actions." Because we had the time to listen to this candidate's story, the knowledge to ask her probing questions, and the expertise to recognize the significance of her actions, we could hear this effective head of school loud and clear.

Imagine how different the outcome could have been. In the standard semifinalist interview, it would have been almost impossible for the candidate to convey this story, much less for the search committee to glean the substance behind it. She might have been able to talk generally about faculty morale and communication. Like all candidates, she might have touched on collaboration and its importance. But the opportunity for her to demonstrate what makes her so special would have been lost in the sea of superficiality.

Absent the probing interview, it is simply too easy for search committees to the "yes" pile. "Cultural fit" meant that "black and Hispanic men were often seen as lacking polish whereas white men who lacked polish were deemed coachable and kept in the running."[5] This is but one example of the subtle stereotyping that takes place among these professionals.

The parallels seem strikingly clear between the studies of Burrell and Rivera on the one hand and the composition and work of independent school search committees on the other hand. As soon as board chairs appoint the search committee, they have sown the seeds of the ultimate selection of a head of school. Rivera makes it clear that those candidates in the "maybe" pile often were moved to "yes" because they had a champion on the committee, someone more like the candidate than anyone else on the committee.[6]

It seems reasonable that having a more diverse search committee will increase the chances that a champion will emerge for the candidate who may not fit the head of school mold but may be exactly what the school needs going forward. Moreover, as stated above, diverse groups tend to make better decisions. The multiplicity of perspectives leads to rich discussion and a more disciplined approach that gravitates to evidence over emotion. Real leadership skills, not just the easy default of cultural fit, have a fighting chance.

---

gravitate to a default that distinguishes candidates on the basis of how well they perform in the interview. In short, interpersonal skills—an important consideration but certainly not the only one—drive decision-making at the expense of other vital leadership skills. Perceptions about cultural fit win the day.

If your school is working with a firm on your search, instruct your consultants to avoid being limited by the time constraints that are typical of first-round group interviews. Instead, ask them to delve into pertinent issues and use follow-up questions to uncover not only candidates' philosophies in action but also their default behaviors and their capacity to learn. Often consultants can leverage their experience as former heads to probe beyond the superficial.

If your school chooses not to use a consultant, we believe it is crucial to modify the process to allow the search committee to ask probing questions about past behavior. In this scenario, the school may choose to have only four or five first-round interviews, as opposed to the typical eight to 10, to allow time to focus on key qualities and skills for each candidate. Worthwhile topics to explore could include communication challenges, difficult decisions, hiring failures, disagreements with the board chair, and examples of times the candidate initiated and implemented change.

Stay Focused on What's Most Relevant

During the finalist stage, the typical search committee gathers feedback about each candidate's interpersonal and communication skills. Given that this feedback usually comes from having each finalist talk to parents, teachers, alumni, students, and trustees in an open search, the search committee is almost guaranteed to receive an abundance of information about each candidate's interpersonal skills.

However, that is why committee members must ensure that they will also receive relevant information on *other previously identified* leadership skills. Focus on a handful of qualities essential for moving the school forward, and design questions that will lead to evidence of the presence or absence of these qualities.

For example, if the committee is probing *initiative*, it might begin with the following topic: "Tell us about your leadership role in a major change initiative." Probing questions could include the following:

- Why was this initiative important?
- What factors contributed to the selection of your team?
- Did you have a fixed outcome in your mind? Explain.
- What research did you conduct?
- Were there dissenting voices on the committee? How did you deal with them?
- How did you maintain the committee's momentum?
- What factors slowed you down? How did you respond?
- How did you share the committee's ongoing work with members of the faculty and staff?
- How did you achieve consensus?
- How did you deal with resistance?
- How did you roll out the plan?
- Did you develop an implementation plan? A communication plan?
- How did you measure the effectiveness of the change?

- Did the change bring about the desired outcomes?
- What did you learn from the experience?

Of course, what's missing from this list are follow-up questions prompted by the candidate's answers. Those are also important. But, in general, your search committee should be looking to uncover evidence that the candidate

- can think strategically;
- can manage the process of change, including dissent;
- has a clear rationale for the kind of outcomes the person wants;
- possesses a political sensibility;
- knows when to push and when to pull back;
- can communicate and execute effectively;
- knows the difference between action and results; and
- is able to gain new insights as a result of the experience.

A CRUCIAL STEP TO A BETTER PROCESS

The process for selecting heads and, in particular, the quality of thinking that informs that process must improve dramatically if independent schools are to thrive and continue to play a vital role in American education.

This section of the *Head Search Handbook* addresses additional important steps to broaden candidate pools and the way committees think about them. But the primary message comes back to this: Trustees, search committees, and consultants can start improving the process by understanding the bias that search committee members bring to the table and then working to mitigate it. Never forget that winning the job is different from doing the job. The more your committee focuses on how a candidate will perform on the job, the greater the chances your school will find its next great leader.

ENDNOTES

[1] Daniel Kahneman, *Thinking, Fast and Slow* (New York: Farrar, Straus & Giroux, 2011).

[2] Ibid.

[3] Lisa Burrell, "We Just Can't Handle Diversity," *Harvard Business Review*, July-August 2016; online at https://hbr.org/2016/07/we-just-cant-handle-diversity.

[4] Ibid.

[5] Lauren A. Rivera, *Pedigree: How Elite Students Get Elite Jobs* (Princeton, NJ: Princeton University Press, 2015).

[6] Ibid.

1. Understand that humans are naturally inclined toward many behavioral biases and that saying so is not a character indictment. Rather, it's a first step toward mitigating them.

2. Recognize, too, that "bias" is not a euphemism for "racism" or "sexism." There are many other types of bias that can affect decision-making.

3. To overcome bias, formulate probing questions that will help your committee steer clear of innate prejudices. Then allow time for interviews that inform rich and extended discussions that lead to evidence over emotion.

10

Reducing Bias in Your Head of School Search

By Ayanna Hill-Gill, Amani Reed, and Kim Roberts

■ Life choices, anxiety about cultural fit, and even hair styles can be obstacles to people of color and white women who aspire to become school heads—unless search committees pay attention to the challenges that unconscious bias can present.

The glass ceiling in independent school leadership was shattered long ago, with women heading independent schools for more than a century and people of color for at least 40 years. Still, NAIS statistics on white women and people of color in headship speak for themselves, as the research discussed in Chapter 8 makes clear.

The issue is not the precedent but the process: Workplace structure, bias, and stereotypical family roles and responsibilities all create a "glass obstacle course" that reveals a more subtle and highly personal set of challenges that are perhaps even more intractable.[1]

As Tia Kathleen Gueye writes in "Race in the Appointment and Daily Leadership of African American Independent School Heads," research has shown that

> although African Americans, other people of color, and women apply to more School Head positions than do Whites, factors such as age, lack of experience as assistant head of school, and geographic limitations result in lower numbers of women and people of color being appointed.[2]

Many of these factors are beyond the immediate control of a search committee. If a candidate needs to live near family or an urban center to balance the demands of a two-career family, for example, there is little a search committee from a rural school can do.

However, many obstacles can be addressed by search committees that are committed to attracting a diverse pool of candidates. This chapter highlights some of these factors and, in particular, the way implicit bias can influence the search process and ultimately a search committee's chance of success in attracting and hiring a white woman or person of color.

HOW BIAS AFFECTS THE CANDIDATE POOL

White women and people of color must often do extra work to convince themselves and others that they are ready for headship. Even the best-intentioned search committees have internalized race- and gender-based beliefs that are subtle and unconscious. For women, the obstacle course is often less connected to a search committee's sense of her competence to lead and more related to her personal life choices—choices that seldom raise questions when candidates are male. Think about it. Given that headship can be close to a 24/7 enterprise, why don't search committee members wonder, "How will he manage the demands of the job while also being a father?" Or what's the likelihood that members would wonder about a single man or a newly married man, "Will he remain fully committed to our school if he decides to start a family?"

Similarly, if a married man does not have children, do committee members think, "Can we really trust him to understand children when he doesn't have any himself?"

Whether directed at men or at women, questions like these are generally unanswerable, often irrelevant, and at times even illegal (see Chapter 11 and its sidebar on legalities). The best thing for search committees to do: Identify the non-negotiable off-the-clock aspects of the role. Then use the interview process to assess whether candidates are still interested once they understand the ways the requirements of the headship role are defined.

For people of color (and, we would argue, working-class women), the bias is twofold:

1. Unless their credentials are impeccable, candidates of color often have difficulty gaining notice from the search firms that serve as gatekeepers in the majority of searches. This can occur not necessarily because the search firms are biased but because they believe their clients are.

2. There is anxiety around cultural fit and school brand for the search committee. A search committee might wonder, "If we were to hire an African-American head, does that mean that we would brand ourselves as a school for African-American students?" Or "While we fully understand and believe in this candidate's excellence, can we count on our community to do the same? Can we still attract full-pay families who might have erroneous notions about race or social status and how they correlate to excellence in leadership?" This can be a particularly challenging set of questions for people of color who embrace cultural dress or "natural" hair.

Most people of color who are currently serving as school heads indicate that they had the following advantage during the search process: The boards of their schools clearly stated diversity as a value before the search began. This suggests that there is a vicious cycle at work. It will be very challenging for a candidate of color to find success in many searches unless the search committee is intentional about its values.

MITIGATING BIAS IN YOUR HEAD SEARCH

The power to build a more diverse population of school heads lies with search committees, and many have articulated a desire to be part of a trend that brings more white women and people of color to headship. The way committees treat and interact with candidates has an impact on how those individuals interact with and understand a school community. With empathy for difference and an understanding of the way they demonstrate their own unintended biases, search committees can mitigate the bias that may be inherent in their behaviors. With bias mitigated, candidates who are white women and people of color will feel more included and respected, thus making the school more attractive for diverse leadership.

Here are some ways in which a committee can make a school's leadership opportunity more appealing to these candidates.

Identify Your Own School's Bias

Taking a lead from the previous two chapters, your search committee must begin the search process by recognizing that biases exist even in the most progressive school communities—including yours. The committee must then mitigate these biases as effectively as possible. Research indicates that many white women and people of color have comparable or even stronger academic backgrounds and qualifications than white male candidates in a pool. However, their credentials are often more heavily scrutinized, and candidates may be identified as high risk within the expectations of a school community on the basis of history and precedent.[3]

Rather than focusing on how a candidate may or may not fit community expectations, your search committee must review candidates' accomplishments and experiences objectively and acknowledge skills that would help the school grow. Too often, decisions regarding cultural fit are influenced by assumptions based on gender, age, and appearance. For example, white women and people of color often experience a different level of scrutiny regarding their physical appearance than others in the candidate pool.

Train the Search Committee

As discussed in the previous chapter, an important way to help search committees lessen demonstrated bias is to diversify the search committee. Once the committee is diversified, providing training for cultural competence in hiring is critical.[4] Training should include an assessment of inclusivity within your school community. If the school itself doesn't embrace diversity as a value, then regardless of the composition of the search committee, retaining a white woman or head of color will be challenging, if not impossible. This training should provide an opportunity to explore questions such as these:

- Does the school's mission statement include a position on diversity?
- How many white women and people of color are in leadership positions at the school?
- What is the number of faculty of color and their retention rate?

It is within the training that the committee needs to identify criteria for candidates and how experience is evaluated. (See Chapter 14.) Discuss candidate diversity early in the process, and if you're hiring a search firm, select the one that best understands and represents your school's values. Within this training, your committee will need to determine its comfort level in reaching outside traditional pools to ensure a wide representation of candidates.

The training should include common ways that bias shows up in hiring and how to overcome it. For example, when people of color are perceived to "skip steps"—like going from being a classroom teacher to a division head—they are scrutinized more closely than when white candidates do the same.

Set Clear Expectations When Choosing Your Search Firm

As discussed elsewhere in this section, if you are selecting a search firm, it is critical to discuss the criteria the firm will use to determine which applicants to share. Make it clear that you want to expand the pool to include candidates who have not been born and bred in independent schools (which have traditionally been white and elite and, therefore, have a smaller candidate pool of people of color). Request proactive outreach by asking the firm to contact other heads of color to recommend qualified candidates. Your search committee can also decide to mandate that white women and people of color be included in the finalist pool as serious candidates.

Mentor and Plan for the Future

Remember that qualified candidates will research each school engaged in a head search to assess what it would be like to live and work in a particular school community. People of color will want to know whether their families would feel safe and welcomed or be treated as outsiders. They will wonder whether they would be living in an isolated location where they are one of very few of their race or ethnicity.

This means that, to recruit more candidates from diverse backgrounds into the head role, ultimately schools themselves must address the pipeline. Not only would every school benefit from a more diverse workforce that reflects its own student population, but the increased diversity would ultimately benefit the independent school profession. By recruiting diverse faculty and staff at every level, but particularly in mid- and senior-level leadership positions, schools can proactively create leadership pipelines that would train promising white women and people of color within their own organizations. With a more robust pipeline, there will be more qualified candidates. And with more qualified independent school candidates—alongside a search committee dedicated to fighting bias—trustees who want to build a more diverse pool of leaders in independent schools will ultimately be successful.

For years, many search committees have told consultants, "We'd like to see a diverse pool." If the consultant can draw white women and people of color to your candidate pool, it is essential that those candidates find a welcoming committee that has been thoughtful about how their behaviors affect the search experience of all types of candidates.

ENDNOTES

[1] Kim Roberts, "Headship and the Glass Obstacle Course," *The Head's Letter*, May 2015.

[2] Tia Kathleen Gueye, "Race in the Appointment and Daily Leadership of African American Independent School Heads" (Dissertation Proposal), Fordham University, New York, 2015, p. 2; online at https://www.nais.org/Articles/Documents/Race%20 in%20the%20Appointment%20and%20Daily%20Leadership%20of%20African%20 American%20Independent%20School%20Heads.pdf.

[3] Sean Thomas-Breitfeld and Frances Kunreuther, *Race to Lead: Confronting the Nonprofit Racial Leadership Gap* (New York: Building Movement Project, 2017); online at http:// www.buildingmovement.org/pdf/RacetoLead_NonprofitRacialLeadershipGap.pdf.

[4] Caroline Sotello Viernes Turner, *Diversifying the Faculty: A Guidebook for Search Committees* (Washington, DC: American Association of Colleges and Universities, 2002); online at https://files.eric.ed.gov/fulltext/ED465359.pdf.

1. Empathize with candidates who are white women and people of color. Realize that they may not be experiencing the search process in the manner that you perceive it and intend for it to be.

2. Given that white males have traditionally held most of the leadership roles at independent schools, be open-minded about nontraditional paths to leadership.

3. Be open with candidates about your school's cultural expectations.

4. Ensure that implicit bias is not at work by continually questioning the assumptions your committee makes about a candidate's readiness or ability to do the job.

5. Seek a candidate, not just a color or gender.

Action Steps for an Inclusive Search Process

By Amada Torres and Caroline G. Blackwell

To improve your process and guarantee a fully inclusive approach, your search committee and search firm can take the following steps to appeal to all candidates.

SEARCH COMMITTEES

- Require all individuals involved in the school's hiring processes to obtain training about implicit bias and cultural competency. These individuals should include staff, trustees, parents, and any external consultants the school engages. (Learn more about training in Chapter 14.)

- Consider asking search committee members to take Project Implicit's test of associations about race, gender, sexual orientation, and other subjects related to social attitudes. It's at https://implicit.harvard.edu/implicit/.

- Ensure that the composition of the search committee includes racial, ethnic, gender, and cultural diversity.

- Determine and agree on job-specific qualifications, and use these criteria to develop a clear position statement that is skill- and knowledge-based.

- Articulate your school's rationale for and commitment to a racially and culturally diverse workforce and candidate pool. Also spell out the ways in which you will fulfill this commitment in your search.

- Establish goals for racial, ethnic, gender, and cultural diversity in your candidate pool. As a minimum standard, remember the Rule of Three: "To have one choice is no choice; to have two choices is a dilemma; and to have three choices offers new possibilities."[1]

- Assess the school's HR policies and procedures to determine whether they match expressed workforce diversity and equity goals.

- Design a uniform process for this search and all others. The process should be transparent and replicable and should use bias-free screening, interview, and evaluative practices. The process should also be subject to accountability reviews.

- Interview search firms in light of your school's commitment to a culturally competent hiring process. Screen out search firms that lack the capacity or willingness to execute a search using the evidence-based criteria and process your school has established.
- Recruit a small, racially and culturally diverse "critical friends-type" search advisory committee to help the school remain accountable to bias-free and bias-mitigating hiring practices and decision-making.

SEARCH FIRMS

First and foremost, search firms are consultative partners who work with client schools to identify, assess, select, and develop education leaders. At their best, search firms commit to, engender, and deliver trustworthiness and expertise throughout a highly professional, diligently monitored process. According to the Association of Executive Search and Leadership Consultants, when considering search firms, you should look for adherence to a Code of Professional Practice that can be summarized in six standards. These standards are integrity, excellence, objectivity, diversity and inclusion, confidentiality, and avoidance of conflicts of interest.[2]

In addition to meeting these standards, the search firms you consider should also have the following:

- A comprehensive database as well as facility with technology and data to drive results
- A proven track record in highly qualified placements
- Demonstrated success in placing candidates whom schools onboard and retain
- A verifiable track record of successfully placing candidates from diverse backgrounds
- Measurable goals for identifying, recruiting, and presenting candidates from diverse backgrounds
- Well-researched assessment and evaluation protocols and tools

ADDITIONAL STRATEGIES

To ensure that your search is fully inclusive, you need evidence-based, proactive strategies for hiring top diverse talent. Research indicates that employers committed to recruiting and retaining racially, ethnically, and culturally diverse employees in business and educational settings go beyond traditional hiring methods to disrupt implicit biases and structural impediments that can foil their goals.[3]

These methods include the following:

- Align your internal search processes and procedures with your school's overall goals.

- Research search firms, as mentioned above, and require demonstrable success in placing white women and people of color in headships and other senior administrative positions.

- Enlist your school's chief diversity officer as a consultant in your hiring process.

- Follow research-based hiring practices.

- Document your search procedures throughout the process, and evaluate your process when your search is completed.

- Create and follow procedural guidelines and checklists to ensure that your hiring process is fair, transparent, and consistent for all applicants.

- Partner with colleges and universities, professional organizations, online search boards, and other digital resources that reach candidates who are historically underrepresented on your campus or in your candidate pools.

- Document your reasons for rejecting finalists, and share the reasons with your search advisory committee.

ENDNOTES

[1] Adrian Segar, "Make Better Decisions With the Rule of Three," Conferences That Work, May 10, 2012; online at http://www.conferencesthatwork.com/index.php/tag/virginia-satir/.

[2] Association of Executive Search and Leadership Consultants, "Code of Professional Practice"; online at https://www.aesc.org/profession/professional-code.

[3] Howard Ross, "Proven Strategies for Addressing Unconscious Bias in the Workplace," CDO Insights, August 2008; online at http://www.cookross.com/docs/UnconsciousBias.pdf.

Evaluating Semifinalists

11

Staying Strategic While Narrowing the Applicant Pool

By Bruce A. Shaw

▨ During this semifinalist stage, design a thorough interview process, stay focused on your selection criteria, and foster candidates' excitement about your school.

When the search for a new head enters the semifinalist stage, your search committee narrows the applicant pool to a much smaller number of individuals to interview. You begin to meet people in earnest, knowing that among them is your next head of school. At this time, you must take care to stay strategic and focused. Your committee members must remain astute judges of potential leaders and right fit while enticing those applicants you want to keep in the pool.

Exactly what takes place at the semifinalist stage can vary widely from school to school. Each school must design a process that works for its own needs and candidate pool. This chapter is geared toward schools that have opted for an open search rather than a closed one, but its essence is relevant to both. In either case, the way your school chooses to conduct the semifinalist stage should be based on your school culture and circumstances as well as such sound practices as these:

1. Design a thorough interview process.
2. Remain focused on the established selection criteria.
3. Market the school effectively.
4. Build connections with candidates.
5. Oversee communications with all constituents.
6. Pay attention to details.

1. DESIGN A THOROUGH INTERVIEW PROCESS

The essential question for your search committee at this point: What process will enable us to learn about candidates' strengths and weaknesses?

At this stage, being intentional about the design process is especially important. Interviews, candidate materials, and reference checks should all be based on defined criteria and provide a thorough, accurate, and three-dimensional picture of each candidate.

The semifinalist round generally includes eight to 10 applicants, and usually only the search committee meets them. It is important to carefully consider what interview venue and style will both help your committee learn about the candidates and send the right message to candidates who are receiving their first—but lasting—impression of the school.

Possible Formats for Interviewing Semifinalists

- Hour-long interviews off campus with the entire search committee
- Search consultant interviews with the candidates the search committee finds most promising, followed by committee interviews with a smaller set of the strongest applicants
- Longer, on-campus, comprehensive interviews with either the full search committee or a portion of the group (followed by full committee interviews later)
- Short on-campus interviews with the entire search committee

The process you choose determines which two or three candidates move forward to the finalist stage. The process should enable a satisfactory answer to the essential question: What process will enable us to learn about candidates' strengths and weaknesses?

When you move to the semifinalist stage and later the finalist stage, an important word in the essential question above is *us*. Your search committee must be clear about which groups and individuals will have access to candidates. In open searches, *us* refers to multiple constituencies who will interact with interviewees and use a survey to provide feedback. In closed searches, *us* refers to a limited group of people, such as the search committee, board members, and small advisory groups.

Good design requires that the search committee, along with the search consultant (if you have one), defines the process. While that process can be modified as circumstances change, it serves as a guide for the interactions that will take place over the next months. It should therefore be clearly understood by both the committee and the candidates, and it needs to be able to be communicated succinctly to the larger community.

As noted earlier, there is no "right" or best practices way of conducting the semifinalist and finalist stages other than designing a process that is *consistent with your school's norms and culture.*

2. REMAIN FOCUSED ON THE ESTABLISHED SELECTION CRITERIA

Now the essential question becomes: What particular competencies does each candidate possess that will strengthen the school over time?

When the search process begins, the new head is a utopian abstraction. Schools and search committees generally describe their next leader as a warm-hearted family person who will nonetheless attend every sporting event, bar mitzvah, and play; a decisive individual of singular vision who also listens intently and collaborates easily; and an external presence and consummate fundraiser who still manages to spend hours daily in classrooms with teachers and kids. Even when following a highly successful head of school, the ideal new person will be different and stronger, possessing gifts the previous head did not.

But in a search, your committee obviously has to meet real people, and you will need to assess them against the set of selection criteria established at the outset of the process. That means you must avoid two major traps.

Major Trap 1: Misplaced focus. As interviews begin, many committees that have spent hours hammering out specific criteria begin to focus on personality. Some committee members like extroverts; others are drawn to those who are less brash. Male and female interviewees often have different styles (as do male and female interviewers). People of color may present differently than their white counterparts, and search committee members may unconsciously project biases. And some candidates are excellent interviewers but, unfortunately, become mediocre heads of school—and vice versa.

To avoid this trap, your search chair needs to be adept at focusing the group on the candidates' competencies in relation to the established selection criteria. Remember that the goal in these initial interviews is to focus on a candidate's expertise and style, and not simply on personality.

Questions to Help Establish Focus

- What are the school's identified needs? (See Chapter 2 on conducting the needs assessment.)
- What skills does each candidate possess that can help leverage the school's strengths, meet challenges, and take advantage of new opportunities?
- How do the candidates' documents, background, and statements back up committee perceptions? In other words, what evidence is there of accomplishment in areas that require that accomplishment?
- How do candidates talk about areas in which they're less skilled, and how can the committee determine their potential in relation to the school's needs?
- What more do committee members need to learn, and how can they learn it?
- How does each candidate's style fit with the school's culture and norms?

Major Trap 2: Misplaced priorities. Too often, this is the point where search committees begin to stray because they unconsciously find themselves choosing people who are unlike the current head in style and personality. Unintentionally elevating those qualities over needed skills, you may become enamored with a person whose talents and style won't meet your school's needs over time.

Avoiding this trap at this stage of interviewing requires tremendous discipline, self-restraint, and self-knowledge.

Every interview should be friendly but rigorous, moving quickly beyond platitudes and superficiality. Resist the common tendency to ask general questions. Instead, frame questions in a way that explains your school. Expect candidates to be analytical in their responses and to invite the kinds of questions strong heads should be asking of the school leaders with whom they will eventually be working.

In other words, don't ask, "How have you been involved with enrollment management at your school?"

Do ask, "As a board, we've been watching the data on enrollment over the past five years and see that families in the areas surrounding the school have less ability to afford an independent school education. As a result, the number of inquiries and applications has started to erode. What has been your experience with enrollment management, and how would you begin to address that issue were you here?"

Suggested Areas for Inquiry and Dialogue During Semifinalist Interviews

- Enrollment management
- Budgeting and finance
- Fundraising
- Program development, curriculum, technology, educational philosophy
- Governance
- Parent relations
- Diversity, equity, and inclusion
- Faculty interactions: professional development, evaluation, support
- Community relations, marketing, and public relations
- Conflict and crisis management

To manage your interviews successfully, start by making sure that your committee is clear about the areas of inquiry that every candidate must address. Then, to make certain the most important ones get asked, assign questions to individual committee members.

Above all, stay fixed on your school's needs and the ways in which individual candidates will (or won't) partner with your school community to meet those needs. During the interviews, listen to how well each person responds to questions related to issues that need to be addressed at your school and also to how well interview answers cohere with a candidate's written materials.

Your search committee will learn a lot about each candidate and, just as important, allow candidates to learn a lot about your school through focused, disciplined questions; dialogue and interchange; explanations about the school's strengths, challenges, and opportunities; and clarity about what the board and school as a whole are seeking. Your goal is to determine fit on both sides.

3. MARKET THE SCHOOL EFFECTIVELY

The essential question: How can we construct a process that will effectively market the school's values, needs, and aspirations?

Wise search committees use every opportunity to talk about the school in such a way that applicants find themselves becoming more and more excited about the possibility of leading it. This requires figuring out not just how you'll learn about your candidates but also how candidates will learn about the school. Your committee should see every interaction and information source as an opportunity to deepen candidates' engagement. With that in mind, ask yourselves:

- What school documents should candidates have, and at what stage of the process should they receive them?
- Whom should candidates meet?
- How can your school show off its classrooms and facilities in a way that communicates your mission, values, and practice?
- How can the process itself engage each candidate intellectually and emotionally with your school's challenges and opportunities so you can build a sense of connection?

4. BUILD CONNECTIONS WITH CANDIDATES

The essential question: How can our search committee build engagement with individual candidates and thus foster their excitement about leading the school?

If you are working with a search firm, in the early stages your consultant is generally the only person who interacts with candidates. But as the search moves into the semifinalist phase, the search committee, and especially its chair, will increasingly become the face and voice of the school. In keeping with the idea that the committee is now working with its next head of school, remember this: Shaping a positive relationship, one that deepens and moves beyond interviewer/interviewee roles, will build a growing sense of affiliation on the part of each candidate.

Before semifinalist interviews, the search chair builds affiliation by making certain that each interviewee understands the schedule and what is expected during the interview. That discussion, which can take place in a phone call, begins to humanize the process.

After the semifinalist interviews, there is usually a lull, but smart search committees stay in touch. The search chair should follow up with all candidates, both those who need to be notified that they are no longer being considered and—most especially—those who are. When contacting the latter, your search chair should be prepared to say why your committee wants the candidate to move forward and how to prepare for the next round.

The design of your search process will determine what interactions take place between the semifinalist interviews and the finalist stage. At some schools, contact may be limited to occasional conversations and the release of documents that will give candidates a fuller understanding of the school. At others, the search may take on a new, more personal dimension designed to deepen connection and understanding. Candidates may interact in person or via Skype with relevant members of the school community, such as the advancement committee, the school's treasurer, or a cohort of faculty involved with a bold new programmatic direction.

Whether the interactions are informal or formal (through, for example, further interviews with segments of the school community), the goal is to engage the finalists by whatever means seem appropriate. By the time finalists begin that phase, each should be excited about the prospect of leading the school, possess a thorough understanding of its challenges and opportunities, and feel welcomed—not just interviewed—by the community. Read more about the finalist stage in Chapters 15 and 16.

5. OVERSEE COMMUNICATIONS WITH ALL CONSTITUENTS

The essential question: How will your search committee provide the candidate interactions the community will expect and use them to buttress the eventual choice for the next head of school?

A search commences with a great deal of activity. Letters go out, a survey is sent, a search consultant or a subset of the search committee spends time on campus meeting with constituents. Then the search goes silent. Because the search committee must keep candidates' names confidential for as long as possible, there is little to communicate beyond process. Your school community needs to understand that and feel confident that all is well despite what can seem like prolonged silence.

The variables in this phase can be tricky. Some candidates are very open about their search for a headship; others would prefer that almost no one know about it. Some school communities have high expectations for involvement; others expect much less. The greatest difficulty comes when a candidate desires confidentiality, perhaps even through the finalist phase, and the community expects involvement.

It is essential to resolve these issues early in the process. You must work closely with your candidates and your search consultant (if you have one) to communicate clearly what your expectations are and to create a well-defined communication plan from the outset. The plan should accomplish three goals:

1. Keep the board of trustees informed throughout and make certain that they understand their unique role and responsibilities.
2. Align with the norms of the school community around constituent involvement in major decisions. (Why does this matter? Think how dif-

ferent a small parent cooperative is from a large boarding school with international students.)

3. Lay the groundwork for the eventual next head of school so that the new leader immediately feels the community's support.

Communicating with the board is especially important. During the confidential phase, not even the board should know the names of the candidates. However, the search committee should make sure that trustees understand the role they will play in interviewing and receive any training or information they need to assess the finalists during the on-campus visits. The search committee should also give trustees plenty of notice about when interviews will take place so they can add them to their personal schedules.

It is vital as well that trustees fully understand how the board will elect its new head. This understanding should include the fact that a final, recorded vote is traditionally unanimous and that announcing a unanimous vote to the community is the first act of support the board provides for the head-elect.

6. PAY ATTENTION TO DETAILS

The essential question: How will you oversee every detail so that the search process reflects well on your school and projects professionalism, organization, and sound management?

The myriad details involved in running a search need to be thought out and completed thoroughly so that all necessary tasks occur seamlessly. These tasks include scheduling interviews, managing communications, providing clear feedback, staying in touch, creating semifinalist and finalist schedules, working with the school's attorney to develop a binding letter of agreement and contract, developing a term sheet for the eventual compensation package, helping candidates with travel arrangements, creating and analyzing constituent surveys, arranging for background checks, coordinating site visits, and keeping board members informed.

The semifinalist stage may not seem to be the most strategic part of a search since its parts are highly tactical. Nevertheless, it fits under the overall strategy of presenting your candidates with a school that is skilled and organized in managing a complex process such as a search. For example, some search firms arrange for all travel arrangements, and the school reimburses the firm rather than the candidate. Other search committees ask candidates to pay their own expenses and ensure that the school reimburses them quickly. Later on, in some finalist interviews, the search committee asks candidates to present to the faculty and the board, to interact with a student group, or to make a longer introduction to parents. In others, the committee only wants candidates to meet select individuals or groups and expects only Q&A.

The point is that each of these decisions needs to be made and then needs to be made very clear to candidates: "This is what you need to prepare. This is how we will be assessing you."

A FOUNDATION FOR STRONG, ENDURING LEADERSHIP

Search committees that follow these steps should find that their searches run smoothly at the semifinalist stage. The key is this: Your interactions with candidates must always center on each person's competence *in relation to a defined set of needs*. Then the process will create both clarity and high expectations, and it will begin to build the kind of strong, professional relationship with the new head of school that your community needs. Following good practices and using strong communication will inspire confidence and support the leadership of the head-elect long before that person arrives on campus.

The search itself should lay a powerful foundation for strong leadership that will last many years and serve the school well.

1. Make sure that, at this semifinalist stage, all your interviews and candidate materials are firmly rooted in the criteria you defined in your position statement and provide a thorough perspective on each candidate.

2. Take steps to avoid being drawn in by attractive personalities or by the urge to hire someone who's the opposite of your current head of school.

3. Show your school to best advantage so that the candidates you most want to attract will be attracted to your school. Doing so requires viewing every interaction as a means to deepen candidates' engagement. It also means managing every detail so that the search process reflects well on the school's professionalism.

The Legalities of Interviewing

By Debra P. Wilson

The interview process allows your committee to really get to know the candidates, including how their experiences will provide a different lens for your school, and it allows the candidates to get to know your school as well. But the interview process is also an area where key legal questions come into play.

Interviewers for your school, including board members, faculty, or parents, need to be aware of the legal limitations on questions that interviewers may ask, even in a casual setting. This can be particularly challenging for head of school searches because when candidates come to campus, their interactions are more formal throughout the day and less formal during meals and social gatherings. Decision-makers need to be aware that, in all of these settings, topics not related directly to the job should not be discussed. Furthermore, if your committee is aware of answers to questions that aren't relevant to the position, the answers cannot be considered when the committee is reviewing the candidate's background and appropriateness for the position. The lists below can be helpful, but all interviewers must think about whether the question being asked, or the information being considered, is related to the actual position.

Additionally, the interview process should be as similar as possible for all candidates. Treating candidates differently by asking different questions or by providing a different experience (scheduling, events, etc.) does not give the committee the opportunity to compare them in a similar light and can raise legal concerns.

TOPICS TO AVOID

Federal law or public policy dictates that some topics are irrelevant to the employment context in almost any employment scenario, and these must not be discussed. Beyond the interview, information related to these characteristics should also not be considered when the committee is discussing whether the candidate is a good fit for the job or at any point in the committee's determination. This is true *even if* the search committee is making a conscious attempt to bring diversity to the position. Unless the school has been required to adopt, or has voluntarily adopted, an affirmative action plan, diversity should not be part of the committee's decision-making process. Committees and interviewers should be careful to avoid questions that try to tease out these topics indirectly as well.

Areas that must be avoided:

- Race or color
- Age
- Ancestry/national origin. This includes asking candidates where they or their parents were born.
- Physical or mental disability. You may ask only whether the candidate can perform the duties of the job in question, with or without reasonable accommodations.
- Veteran status
- Military discharge type
- Height or weight restrictions. These topics can be used to screen for other protected classes and are therefore not open to consideration.
- Pregnancy
- Genetics. Genetics includes both the individual's genetic testing or any genetically related illness or diagnoses and those of family members.
- State and local protected categories. Schools must remain abreast of limitations that state or local governments may add to this list. These often include discrimination related to transgender applicants, sexual orientation, etc.

Areas that may be considered in some circumstances:

- Financial status. Schools may not ask candidates about their financial status, but they can use consumer credit reports when such reports are relevant to the position in question (as is the case with a head of school).
- Religion. Religion may be considered by religious schools that give a preference to candidates of the school's religion.
- Citizenship status. Schools may ask whether the individual is eligible to work in the United States.
- Sexual orientation and transgender applicants. Religious schools occasionally find that sexual orientation can be an issue in their hiring decisions. At the time of writing, there is no blanket federal law that precludes schools from discriminating on the basis of sexual orientation or gender identification. But all schools should be aware that, as of when this book was published, the

Equal Employment Opportunity Commission (EEOC) has been trying to find ways to include discrimination on the basis of sexual orientation and gender identification under other federal laws in various lawsuits. This activity has continued under the Trump administration. Many state and local governments have also been very active in this area. Schools asking questions or using information in their selection process should be very aware of the relevant laws in this area.

SALARIES

Some states, such as Massachusetts, Oregon, and Delaware, and locales such as New York City and Philadelphia, have moved quickly to forbid employers to ask about salary history. The reasoning behind this prohibition is that salary history can work against women in the employment and salary-setting process. Schools should be aware of local and state laws in this area before asking for previous salary histories from candidates.

A WORD ON CRIMINAL RECORDS

In 2012, the EEOC released guidance into the practice of employers considering arrest and conviction records. State and local authorities have also been delving into this issue. For schools, convictions can be very relevant to a candidate's suitability for a position, given the high level of trust and responsibility required to work with children. Questions relating to a candidate's arrest record may not be asked. However, schools may consider a candidate's conviction record if the record is relevant to the position, and they frequently do so. If your school is considering conviction records, the committee must consider the following:

- The nature and gravity of the offense
- The amount of time that has passed since the offense and/or the completion of the sentence
- How the offense and the amount of time that has passed relate to the nature of the job in question

WHAT *CAN* WE ASK?

Any questions relevant to the position are generally fair game. The committee will most likely want to get a feel for candidates and what kind of leaders they are, as well as how they perceive the match between school and skills. Common questions include the following:

- Describe a time when you made a wrong decision. What did you learn from it, and how did it shape you as a leader?
- We are a small but growing school, and financial management is very important to this position. What experiences have you had that might help us in this area?
- Diversity and inclusion are core to our school's mission. What work have you done in these areas in the past, and what opportunities do you see for us?
- Do you have any reservations about this position?
- What excites you most about education?
- What are your key strengths as a leader? What are your key weaknesses?
- Is there anything we have not asked that you wish to share with us?

Search committees should remember that the interview process is a way for them to get to know the candidates and for the candidates to get to know the school and community. It is OK if the candidates offer information that should not be asked about in the interviews, but the information should not be considered when the committee is making decisions about the candidate selection.

Don't try to solve the algorithm. Because they face a hiring decision outside their usual fields of expertise, search committee members are sometimes inclined to "score" candidates. Figuratively speaking, they want to use a formula to ascribe numerical values to criteria such as degrees earned, the prominence of schools served, and competence in skills such as fundraising or curriculum development. These criteria may help define some qualifications. But whether to appoint a candidate should depend ultimately on qualitative judgments about the person's preparedness for the position and ability to inspire constituents by force of intellect, gravitas, and alignment with culture and mission.

Linc Eldredge, President, Brigham Hill Consultancy

Remember that a search is not a popularity contest. It is really easy to be swayed by personality alone. Of course, affability is helpful, but you are not hiring the person you'd most like to talk to at a cocktail party. Keep going back to the objective criteria as you evaluate candidates. Form a clear understanding of the work that needs to be done, and then hire someone with the skills to do it.

Skip Kotkins, Senior Consultant, Carney, Sandoe & Associates

Focus on candidate experiences—successes and failures—that relate to the challenges and opportunities at hand. It is easy to be carried away by the narrative of what one *could* do, rather than what one *has* done. But it's better to qualify based on action and experience than on hypotheticals. Ask yourself: What issues is this person being hired to address, and what has she or he done that directly relates?

Robin Tweedy, former Senior Consultant, Carney, Sandoe & Associates

12

Using Assessment Tools to Identify Leadership Potential

By Donna Orem

■ A new class of predictive analytic tools known as behavioral assessments attempts to bring some science to the art of hiring.

A crystal ball that could accurately predict best fit for job and culture would be a handy tool for any employer. Getting a hire wrong, particularly when it is the top leadership position, costs an organization time and resources and can damage its position with its constituents.

Although there are no silver bullets in the hiring process, there is a new class of predictive analytic tools, known as behavioral assessments, that attempts to bring some science to the art of hiring. These tools forecast preferences and behavior in an effort to better match candidates with needed skills and abilities for the job and workplace culture. Industrial psychologist Todd Harris notes in *Inc.* magazine that these behavioral assessments can bring perspective, balance, and fairness into the hiring process. Too often, he suggests, the hiring process is about "likes" rather than "needs."[1] Behavioral assessments can help a search committee home in on current organizational needs with some precision. Getting those needs identified correctly is the first step in ensuring that an organization is hiring the right candidate for the job to be done.

Hiring a head of school is both an art and a science. Throughout this book, we discuss planning and processes that can ensure an artful execution. In this chapter, we will explore how adding a bit of science to the mix can bring new insights to the process and offer a set of checks and balances to other parts of the hiring process.

HISTORY OF BEHAVIORAL ASSESSMENTS

The idea of predicting behavior by assessing personality traits dates back at least to ancient Greece, when Hippocrates advanced the theory that one's behavior can be linked to four distinct temperaments (sanguine, choleric, melancholic, and phlegmatic). The 20th century brought forward many new theories, including Freud's three components of the mind (id, ego, and superego) and Jung's categories of mental functioning (sensing, intuition, thinking, and feeling). Jung's theories spawned one of the first attempts to create a test around personality theories, the Myers-Briggs Type Indicator. Since then, the world of behavioral assessments has flourished, with new tools coming to market frequently.

Behavioral assessments have long been a staple of corporate sector hiring. According to research conducted by the Aberdeen Group, 57 percent of companies use behavioral assessments to hire top talent.[2] Education has been slower to adopt the practice of using these tools, but that may be changing. Interest in these tools is increasing in the world of colleges and universities, according to Jessica Kozloff, president of the higher education search firm Academic Search. In an article in *Inside Higher Ed,* she explains, "That's likely because search committees want candidates to possess an ever-broadening set of skills." More and more governing boards are "equally concerned about evaluating the soft skills of somebody, as well as trying to evaluate the hard skills."[3] That kind of in-depth analysis is becoming harder to do with traditional interviewing and reference-checking tools, so the sector is looking to other means of gleaning this information.

Like higher education, the independent school community has not yet fully embraced using behavioral assessments in the search process. In selecting heads of schools, schools generally make experience as a head the chief proxy for the ability to lead effectively. With the forecasted retirement of scores of baby-boomer heads in the coming years, behavioral assessments may become a more useful tool, particularly in evaluating the leadership potential of candidates who have never held a top role. For those who have held previous headships, an assessment can provide insight into a candidate's leadership style and the kind of match that style would be with a school's culture. Finally, for a new hire, the insights gleaned from using behavioral assessment tools can be invaluable in the onboarding process.

GETTING STARTED

Before beginning with a behavioral assessment tool, consider these key steps to ensure that it is used to full potential. First, your committee should weave the use of behavioral assessment tools into the larger search process. These tools are not designed to be used alone and must be integrated into a well-defined process to ensure accurate results. When used appropriately, they can help predict leadership approaches, identify areas for probing through structured interview processes, and provide crucial information for best onboarding a new head. When used inappropriately, they can lead to faulty decision-making or legal challenges of discrimination.

If your school has elected to work with a search firm, that company may have already integrated a particular assessment into its search process. If not, there are many good tools on the market from which to choose. Early in the search process, your search committee should discuss with the search firm how and at what stage in the process the assessment will be used. Most of the high-quality tools on the market will provide explicit advice on how the tool is best implemented.

Selecting a Tool

For employment purposes, behavioral assessments are generally online exams with no wrong or right answers, just preferences, or with questions that prompt some self-reflection. But because behavioral assessment tools are designed for different processes, choosing the right one is crucial. Before you move forward with any of the tools on the market, industrial psychologist Harris suggests taking the following steps:

1. Identify what the assessment is designed to measure and accomplish and how it will benefit the school. Some assessments are designed for selection; others are best used for growth and development.

2. Investigate whether the assessment comes with an accompanying job analysis that allows for a thorough identification of a job's requirements—crucial for the search process.

3. Ensure that the tool has been tested for bias and that documentation is available confirming that the assessment is free of bias with respect to the respondent's age, gender, race, ethnic group, etc.

4. Ensure that the assessment has been tested for validity and reliability. This kind of testing should prove that the assessment can predict important workplace behaviors and that a person's results are consistent and repeatable over time.[4]

Types of Tools

There are many behavioral assessments on the market today. Here's a look at a sampling of them.

Perhaps the best known is the *Predictive Index*.[5] Within its stable of tools, there are a number of assessments available for the search process:

- **Job assessment.** Key stakeholders who will interact with the position take this assessment to generate an ideal behavioral and cognitive target.
- **Behavioral assessment.** Candidates take this assessment, which measures core behavioral drivers. The results can help the search committee in the screening process.
- **Cognitive assessment.** This provides insight into a person's cognitive ability or learning aptitude, helping the committee determine an individual's capacity to learn, adapt, and grasp new concepts in the workplace. This can be key information in making hiring decisions for a top leadership job.

NAIS uses the *Omnia* tools[6] in both its selection process and staff development. Like the Predictive Index, Omnia offers both cognitive and job assessments, as well as a host of tools that can be used for onboarding and team performance. Omnia's Leadership Report can identify a leader's individual style and bring self-awareness to how that style affects relationships and school culture.

Emotional intelligence (EQ) plays a key role in effective school leadership, and there are a number of assessments that measure EQ along a variety of different scales. The *Emotional and Social Competence Inventory*,[7] although more appropriate for development than selection, works as a 360-degree assessment to help leaders understand their EQ and build on their capabilities.

Management POP,[8] a selection tool, measures an individual's potential for success and sustainability as a manager or leader, including assessment of

- personality traits as they apply to management roles;
- leadership style and approach;

- comfort with conflict; and
- self-confidence, emotional intelligence, and people orientation.

In January 2002, NAIS used this instrument to identify the traits very successful school heads held in common and found that emotional intelligence was at the top of the list.

Avoiding Legal Challenges

Some organizations have been hesitant to use behavioral assessment tools because there have been incidences of litigation. Specifically, there have been recent challenges that some tools discriminate against those with mental disabilities. The Omnia Group outlines a number of steps a school must take to avoid challenges:

- Make sure to keep the assessment relevant to what your school is trying to accomplish. When hiring, use only assessments that are strictly designed for that purpose.
- Don't make the test results the sole basis of a hiring decision. The assessment should be just one part of a well-thought-out hiring process and an additional information source among many relating to your candidates.
- As mentioned above, make sure that the instrument has been screened for bias and tested for validity and reliability and that there is documentation.[9]

INTEGRATING BEHAVIORAL ASSESSMENTS INTO THE SELECTION PROCESS

Because the job of head of school has become increasingly complex, finding the right fit for the position and the school culture can be daunting. The successful search committee will conduct thoughtful planning up front, have a clear vision and values statement, develop a well-defined timeline, and decide at the outset whether behavioral assessment tools can help in the search. Whatever process a search committee decides on for assessing candidates' abilities, the result is most likely to be positive when there are multiple inputs, using both artful and scientific approaches, to ensure that information is reliable.

ENDNOTES

[1] Kay McFadden, "7 Tips for Using Personality Tests to Hire," *Inc.* magazine, March 21, 2011; online at http://www.inc.com/guides/201103/7-tips-for-using-personlity-tests-to-hire.html.

[2] Amy Gulati, "Selecting, Using Hiring Assessments to Optimal Effect," Society for Human Resource Management, May 11, 2015; online at https://www.shrm.org/ResourcesAndTools/hr-topics/talent-acquisition/Pages/Selecting-Using-Hiring-Assessments.aspx.

[3] Kellie Woodhouse, "Presidential Personality," *Inside Higher Ed*, August 28, 2015; online at https://www.insidehighered.com/news/2015/08/28/more-presidential-searches-embrace-personality-assessments.

[4] McFadden, "7 Tips."

[5] The Predictive Index (PI); online at http://www.predictiveindex.com/.

[6] The Omnia Group; online at http://www.omniagroup.com/.

[7] Emotional and Social Competence Inventory (ESCI); online at http://www.eiconsortium.org/measures/eci_360.html.

[8] Management POP; online at https://www.selfmgmt.com/products/assessments-selection-tools/management-pop/.

[9] Crystal Spraggins, "Are Employee Behavioral Assessments Legal?" Omnia Group, March 1, 2014; online at http://www.omniagroup.com/are-behavioral-assessments-legal/.

TOP TIPS

1. Recognize that there are scientific avenues to assess whether a candidate matches the position description.

2. Decide whether your committee wants to use a behavioral assessment and, if so, which tool will garner the information you are seeking.

3. Be sure the way you apply the assessment tool meets legal requirements.

4. Understand that behavioral assessments are best applied within a broader context that respects the individual's background and unique characteristics.

5. If you decide to use an assessment, design the selection process so that the results can be used as intended.

13

A Model for Measuring Skills, Experience, and Fit

By Rosa-Lyn Morris

> ■ Recruiters have developed numerous models, maps, and tools to organize the process of evaluating candidates. This chapter spells out a model that frames the assessment of skills, experience, and fit.

As noted in Chapter 12, choosing a new head of school is both an art and a science. And the stakes are high: Just as a wise hire can launch your school on a trajectory to greatness, a bad one can cost your school time, resources, and standing in the community.

Having a thorough, structured evaluation process that assesses skills, experience, and fit is crucial to helping your search committee make the best possible decision. These search criteria should drive the evaluation process, from the writing of the position description and job application to the development of your search timeline. Every step and round of the process should be planned to help your committee assess one or more of your search criteria.

ONE ASSESSMENT MODEL

Recruiters have developed numerous hiring models, maps, and tools to organize and structure the process. This chapter uses the Korn Ferry 4D (Four Dimensions) model to frame the assessment of skills, experience, and fit.

The Four Dimensions, as explained on the Korn Ferry website (http:// www.kornferry.com/kf4d/kf4d), "measure attributes of individuals that are more readily visible as well as those that are harder to see and critical to someone's career decisions and behavior." These are the four attributes:

1. **Competencies**, the essential ingredients of success at work, distilled into observable skills and behaviors.

2. **Experiences**, the previous assignments or roles that prepare a person for future opportunities.

3. **Drivers**, the deep internal values, motivations, and aspirations that influence a person's choices. They can be specific or broad and can fluctuate based on the person's circumstances and stage of life.

4. **Traits**, the personality characteristics that influence behavior. They include attitudes, such as optimism or confidence, and natural leanings such as social astuteness.[1]

There are many ways to evaluate a candidate's competencies through careful examination of experience and behavioral interviewing. But when your goal is to hire a new head for a long tenure, it's important to successfully evaluate traits and drivers, which factor into the candidate's fit. As consultants often say, "Leaders are hired for what they know and fired for who they are." This chapter will explore best practices and options for the candidate evaluation process in all four of these dimensions.

FITTING ASSESSMENT INTO THE SEARCH PROCESS

Numerous factors will affect the timeline of your search and sequence of steps, including the resources you have available, the composition of the search committee, and whether you are using a consultant. Typically, one or two paper evaluations are followed by behavioral and follow-up interviews and reference checks.

The Position Description's Ongoing Importance

As described in Chapter 7, the position description is developed at the beginning of the search process, and your whole school community should have opportunities to provide input on what type of leader is wanted and needed given your school's culture and context. Different climates require different types of leaders—such as the turnaround leader, the status-quo leader, or the change agent—and your board and search committee must find consensus on the qualities, experiences, style, and fit needed for a leader to succeed. The committee should refer to the position description at every stage of the evaluation process, both as a search best practice and to keep the committee on track.

Paper Evaluation

Your first evaluation is a review of paper or electronic submissions/applications, so you'll want to be sure to ask all applicants not only for a resume but also for something that will allow the committee to gauge the applicant's writing. Traditionally, cover letters are used as a writing sample, but they are hard to standardize and evaluate without some direction. Instead, consider asking candidates to answer a brief set of questions that address motivation, experience, and successes and that provide some context about previous mandates and environments where they worked. Your committee should agree on the four or five questions to be asked and set a page limit; the questions should be generated from the agreed-upon position description.

Here's an example of a possible questionnaire:

General Questions

1. Why are you interested in this position at this point in your career?
2. What do you see as the biggest opportunities and challenges facing our school over the next five years?
3. Please provide specific examples of your experience managing a diverse set of stakeholders with competing interests.
4. Please describe your approach to ensuring diversity and inclusion within your current organization. Have these approaches been successful? On reflection, is there anything you would approach differently in the future?
5. Please describe the most innovative project/program that you have led to date.

Context Questions

6. What is the largest team you have ever managed, and at which organization?
7. What is the largest budget you have managed, and at which organization?

During the paper evaluation stage, you're mainly assessing experience—the positions, titles, and educational credibility of a candidate's career. Through the writing activity, your committee can also begin to evaluate competencies required in the position description through leadership behaviors.

It's important to remember that you are not choosing your next leader at this point; you are choosing candidates about whom you want to learn more on the basis of their experiences and competencies. To better inform your final choice, you'll want a wide range of candidates. The more diverse (in background, title, gender, ethnicity, stage of career, etc.) the group of candidates you advance to the semifinal round, the better final decision you will make as a committee.

The Behavioral Interview

After you've conducted the paper evaluation and narrowed down your pool, the next step is to evaluate candidates' competencies through behavioral interviews. A behavioral assessment takes into consideration past behavior in order to predict future behavior. There are several ways to conduct interviews, including in person or via videoconference or telephone. But for leadership positions, it's ideal to conduct in-person interviews whenever possible. Although this stage is time-consuming, the search committee should set a time frame and commit to seeing all the candidates who are moving forward through the process.

For behavioral interviews, your committee should devise a standard set of questions to ask all candidates but remain flexible enough to ask follow-up questions about individual applicants' experience or responses. Chapter 14 provides a detailed approach to formulating solid behavioral interview questions, a process you can apply to all areas of leadership, not just cultural competency. Good topics to cover include leadership/vision, motivation, background/prior experience, people and financial management, external presence/fundraising, and specific mission-related questions based on your school's culture.

Focus your behavioral questions on revealing candidates' leadership styles, accomplishments, talents, skills, values, etc., by asking for relevant examples of their work. Avoid questions that will elicit philosophical answers instead of more meaningful ones rooted in experience.

For example, instead of "What is your vision for XXX School?" ask, "Describe a time you've had to lead a vision/strategic planning process for an organization, department, or major project. What were the mandate and context of the conversation, and what was the outcome?"

And in place of "What is your management style?" ask, "Tell us about a time when you've had to manage competing interests in order to change a policy or program. What does this example tell us about your management style?"

The Second Interview

The second interview is very often conducted at the school and is purposefully less scripted. The goal is to get to know the candidates, including in a social setting, and to see their presentation style. The committee should either decide on a topic and ask each candidate to prepare a presentation in advance or build a case study question relevant to the school's current environment and ask candidates for their impromptu responses.

References

Your evaluation continues as you call the references. Your committee should request a combination of both primary and secondary references, which gives you a 360-degree view of the candidate from supervisors, colleagues, direct reports, and external mentors. Reference questions should probe the candidates' positive leadership behaviors and validate the experience your committee has had with each candidate.

At this point, you are listening for red flags and for patterns of behavior, both positive and negative. If you're working with a search firm, your consultants can help listen and connect the dots to identify behavioral patterns.

The people candidates choose to list as references can sometimes reveal more than what the references say. For example, your committee should notice whether candidates include references who have served as their supervisors, board members, and pertinent external stakeholders; what the chosen references reveal about the level at which the candidates have been working; and whether candidates exclude references from organizations where they have recently been employed. What your committee observes could indicate the need for secondary referencing.

THE EVALUATION PROCESS

The Evaluation Grid

The evaluation grid you use throughout this process should correlate with the job description in each area that the interview process covers; this same step can be converted into a survey if and when the broader community engages in the process. Here's an example of an evaluation grid.

	Candidate 1	Candidate 2
Connection to the School/Motivation		
Leadership, Strategy, and Vision		
Emotional Intelligence and Experience Managing Multiple Stakeholders		
Team Development/Management Experience		
Thought Leadership		
Communication Style/Presence		

RATING CODE: 3=Outstanding; 2=Meets Target; 1=Needs Development; 0=Reservations

Your committee can use the evaluation grid for quantitative measures of assessment, as indicated in the rating code. Note, however, that there is no column for totaling the points. That's because you can't boil down experience, competencies, and fit into a single score. Instead, you should combine your quantitative evaluation of each candidate with qualitative impressions. Qualitative impressions should fit into three groups: strengths, weaknesses, and additional questions. If your committee uses a set of behavioral interview questions derived from the position description, at each stage of assessment you should use the resulting list of strengths, weaknesses, and additional questions to decide which candidates should move forward in the process.

Candidate Fit

As noted in Chapter 12, a growing number of organizations use science as part of leadership assessment. The Korn Ferry 4D tool used in this chapter is a leadership assessment embedded in an executive search process; it allows for further investigation of a candidate's traits and drivers.

The purpose of a leadership tool is to enhance the experience you're having with a candidate and provide further areas for investigation. But a natural question for your committee members to ask themselves is, "When will we know that a particular person is a fit for us?"

As a community and committee, ignite that honest discussion at the outset of the search by determining key characteristics you're looking for beyond experience and competencies. To define fit for your school, begin with an assessment of your school's current culture. Ask, for example: Is your school's culture innovative, structured, traditional, or collaborative? Is the school's environment stable, in crisis, or characterized by an appetite for change? Is there a mission-critical trait a candidate needs for credibility in the community—a trait related to your school's single-gender or religious mission or to international experience? This dialogue will enable the committee to evaluate fit either by using a leadership tool or by watching for identified characteristics during the interview process. Of course, the cultural-fit characteristics you identify should also be included in the position description.

Here are some questions that should elicit answers that will help you evaluate fit—key traits and drivers of an individual—if you aren't employing a leadership tool. (These questions could be used in addition to a leadership tool, of course.)

- Describe a failure in your professional career. This failure should be something for which you had ultimate responsibility. How did you handle the failure, and what have you learned from it?
- What defining event or moment put you on a trajectory to become a head of school?
- How do you recharge your battery during a stressful or busy time in your professional work?
- What is the book (either from your field or from the world of literature or philosophy) that has had the most profound impact on you—either changing the way you viewed the world or altering your understanding of your role in it?

Just as you can learn a lot about teachers by observing how they present their lessons, observing how leaders treat other people is more powerful than simply asking them what they do. If you're using a search consultant, the consultant can provide insight into how the candidate behaves outside the formal evaluating environment. For example, watching a candidate's behavior when a plane is delayed or a hotel needs to make a room change can reveal a great deal. This kind of informal evaluation can be used to inform reference questions and identify a pattern of behavior that would not be a good fit.

Last but not least, make sure your committee members follow this simple but powerful advice: Trust your gut. Your committee is made up of individuals who care deeply about the history and future of your school; their insights can be quite telling. Although gut instinct should by no means be the only tool for evaluating fit, it should not be overlooked.

THE IMPORTANCE OF MULTIFACETED ASSESSMENT

The ultimate message is this: Your search committee should not rely on just one mode of assessment. Evaluating candidates' skills, experience, and fit requires a multifaceted approach. This includes using your position description as a consistent evaluation tool, assessing resumes and writing exercises, conducting behavioral interviews, employing leadership tools when available, checking references, and observing candidates in as many different contexts as possible throughout the vetting process.

ENDNOTE

[1] "Korn Ferry's Four Dimensions of Leadership and Talent"; online at https://www. kornferry.com/kf4d/kf4d.

1. Realize that your position description is *the key evaluation tool* at every stage of the vetting process.

2. Seek to answer two questions about candidates: (1) What do they do? (as defined through leadership competencies and experiences and assessed through resumes, writing, and interviews) and (2) Who are they? (which is harder to assess without a leadership tool that takes into consideration the candidate's personality traits and drivers).

3. Evaluate experiences and competencies through a behavioral interview that takes into consideration past behavior in order to predict future behavior.

4. Assess skills, experience, and fit through both quantitative (rating grid) and qualitative (committee dialogue) measures. The qualitative impressions should fit into three groups: Strengths, Weaknesses, and Additional Questions.

5. Use reference checks to validate experience, competencies, and personality traits. As a committee, use references to help you identify both positive and negative patterns of behavior.

6. Remember that candidate fit is one of the best predictors of success and that determining fit begins with a cultural assessment of the

school itself. Embed those cultural characteristics within the job description, and then evaluate fit through formal and informal techniques, including behavioral interviews, referencing, and a leadership tool.

7. Recognize that although instinct is not a tool in and of itself, your committee members should trust their gut when assessing candidate fit.

14

Evaluating Cultural Competence

By Cris Clifford Cullinan

Specialized tools and templates can help distinguish between candidates who may be able to speak knowledgeably about cultural competence and those with demonstrated skills in grappling with complex cultural issues.

As the most visible and powerful leader in the school, your next head will set the standard for cultural competence. This individual will be the face, spirit, and character of the school community and must therefore understand how to develop and maintain meaningful inclusion of all stakeholders. As a result, cultural competence should be woven throughout the new head's attributes, skills, and responsibilities.

There is no simple cultural assessment tool to administer to candidates to predict how they will behave on the job. Assessment takes work. But the payoff from that work will be a better hiring process for the search committee and a more successful leader for the school.

This chapter looks at four specific tools and templates that can help a search committee evaluate potential heads' actual experience, knowledge, and skills in dealing with issues of cultural differences, identities, and histories. The approach puts these in the forefront of an effort to discern between two types of candidates: the ones who talk a good game in terms of really valuing or caring about diversity; and those with the demonstrated skills and abilities to act with insight, judgment, and careful thinking when faced with education's complex cultural issues. The approach is designed to provide your search committee with specific examples of experience rather than aspirational statements of what a candidate believes or values.

A CRITICAL IMAGINING PROCESS

Does your search committee know how a culturally competent candidate and a non-culturally competent candidate differ in knowledge and skills?

At the beginning of this process, before looking at candidate information, members of your search committee should imagine that they have chosen two final candidates: Candidate A, who is culturally competent, and Candidate B, who is not. Using easel paper to capture the discussion points, the committee should discuss the following questions:

- What knowledge and skills is Candidate A likely to have that Candidate B will not?
- What leadership experiences is Candidate A likely to have that Candidate B will not?

These lists will be different depending on the school and the issues that are most prominent in terms of cultural differences, identities, and challenges. Table 1 is one example of a list from an urban pre-K-12 school.

QUESTION ANALYSIS PROCESS

Are you asking candidates to tell you what they actually know how to do?

The process above will result in active discussion about what a culturally competent candidate will bring to the school, and such a discussion will help your search committee develop a shared vision of pertinent knowledge, skills, and experience. How do you then develop questions to evaluate candidates in these areas?

Concentrate on writing questions that provide candidates with clear opportunities to explain their experience in areas related to cultural competence. These questions must be both focused and sufficiently complex so that answers can be definitive.

When developing and asking questions related to knowledge and experience, keep in mind that the most effective ones ask candidates how they have used such knowledge in the past and how they would apply, use, and adapt it at your school. For questions related to skills and experience, ask candidates what they did in certain situations, what they learned in the process, and how they would apply that knowledge at your school. Alternatively, pose a realistic situation that a head of school might face, and ask candidates specific questions about how they would handle it.

Table 1: How Two Candidates Could Differ

Head of School Candidate A: *Culturally Competent Knowledge, Skills, and Experience*	Head of School Candidate B: *Deficits in Culturally Competent Knowledge, Skills, and Experience*
• Has knowledge of and experience with the ways socioeconomic class intersects with issues of race and ethnicity in an independent school community	• Is unable to demonstrate experience with, understanding of, or ability to deal with the complex intersections of socioeconomic class with race and ethnicity in the school community
• Has knowledge of—and skills and experience with overseeing—hiring processes for culturally competent faculty and staff	• Is unable to describe how, in a hiring process, the candidate would evaluate the cultural competence of potential faculty
• Has skills and experience in recognizing when school policies, procedures, and practices can act as roadblocks to equity and meaningful inclusion for students and parents from underrepresented groups	• Has little or no experience evaluating and updating school policies, procedures, and practices to ensure that they further equity and inclusion inside and outside of the classroom
• Has knowledge, skills, and experience providing leadership to ensure that all students—and particularly underrepresented students (e.g., young women in science)—have full access to the school's educational opportunities	• Has little or no knowledge, understanding, or experience in mentoring faculty to increase equity, inclusion, and student success for underrepresented students
• Has skills and experience providing leadership and leading dialogue among school administrators, faculty, parents, and other members of the school community to build more inclusive pedagogical processes	• Has little or no interest, skills, or experience creating and leading dialogue among members of the school community, including stakeholders from underrepresented groups, to enhance the educational experience for all students

Consider the following examples of ineffective and effective questions related to a head's cultural competence.

KNOWLEDGE Questions

Ineffective: Why are diversity and equity important factors to consider at independent schools?

Effective: Please provide three distinct examples of how issues of race, ethnicity, color, and socioeconomic class can negatively impact the educational process in independent schools. How would you address these issues as head of this school, given what you know of its history and culture? What past experiences inform your answer?

EXPERIENCE Questions

Ineffective: In the past, have you led conversations, dialogues, or processes about equity issues in an educational setting? How successful were these?

Effective: Please provide two specific examples of when you have played a leadership role in bringing together members of the school community to discuss and resolve equity issues. For each example, please explain the following:

- The basic situation and how you became aware of it
- What leadership role you played in the process
- How you chose and involved stakeholders in the process
- The outcome of the process, your assessment of its success, and the metrics by which you measure that success
- What you learned from this process and how you believe you would use what you learned as our head of school

SKILL Questions

Ineffective: What skills do you see as necessary for a head of an independent school to deal with diversity and equity issues? Explain how you have developed these skills.

Effective: Like all independent schools, ours works to ensure the best possible education for all students. Our student body is more diverse now than it was 10 years ago, especially in terms of ... [provide a list that reflects whatever areas are primary for your school, including race, ethnicity, nationality, gender identity and gender expression, socioeconomic class and class status, etc.]. Please describe at least three leadership skills you would bring to our position and how you would use each to ensure that we continue to improve our educational climate and success for all students.

In each of these pairs, the effective questions ask the candidates to be specific, provide examples, and address how their knowledge, experience, and skills will benefit the school.

Asking any of these effective questions will provide your committee members with specific information to evaluate candidates' readiness to help move the school forward in areas of equity and inclusion. In addition, answers to these questions will yield information about candidates' judgment and decision-making, as well as community-building and leadership skills.

To provide candidates with time to give full consideration to their answers to these complex questions, a best practice is to provide each candidate with a copy of the interview questions at least 30 minutes before the interview. This will offer time for the "adrenalin flood" of the brain to diminish and allow both candidates and interviewers to use the in-interview time more effectively.

THE QUESTION DEVELOPMENT TEMPLATE

Do you know the components of good questions and answers?

One way to bring together the thinking of the committee when considering how to evaluate cultural competence is to outline the following six topics in a single template.

- The specific area or description of cultural competence
- Knowledge related to this area
- Skills and abilities related to this area
- Potential knowledge and experience question(s)
- Potential skills and experience question(s)
- Components sought in a good answer

This last point—identifying the components of a good answer—asks committee members to identify what each expects to hear in an answer. The resulting discussion often results in rewriting and refining the original question. Discussing expectations ahead of time can also lessen the possibility that, during post-interview discussions, the committee discovers that some members thought an answer was excellent but others found it to be lacking basic information. Table

2 illustrates how this information can be laid out on one page after a search committee discussion.

DOCUMENTATION OF CANDIDATE ANSWERS AND EVALUATION OF THOSE ANSWERS

Do you know how to assess candidates on the basis of the substance of their answers rather than on biases that can taint the hiring process?

Even when you ask effective questions, it is possible, and even likely, that poor search committee documentation and lack of clear evaluation criteria can sabotage the process and undercut an outstanding candidate. This is true even when the issues involved do not include cultural competence. So when your committee attempts to gauge a potential head's knowledge, skills, and experience in dealing with issues of difference, discrimination, harassment, equity, and inclusion, it is imperative to guard against a sloppy process. There are several key reasons for this.

1. Everyone is subject to cultural biases. It's imperative to work to ensure clear and honest discussion of candidates' value to the school and resist falling into stereotypical thinking.

2. It is likely that few, if any, members of your search committee or board of trustees have had to answer such complex questions in their own interviews. One reason members are sometimes reluctant to even ask specific questions about culturally competent leadership is that they may not think that they could answer such questions themselves.

3. If your board and search committee have done a thorough job of discussing issues that are relevant to culturally competent leadership, then well-crafted questions and careful evaluation of candidates' responses are more likely. This is important because such committees are composed of very busy people who may tend to look for shortcuts, feel reluctant to engage in complex discussions, and fall back on questions that don't actually pertain to the issues your school is facing.

4. In their typical processes, few search firms include a substantial look at candidates' experience, knowledge, and skills in culturally competent leadership. If your school has used a firm to narrow the candidate field, you may have already lost some good prospects. Carefully consider those remaining in terms of what each would bring to the school to deal with equity and inclusion challenges and to build on opportunities.

Table 2: Question Development Template Example

Essential Function/Description of Specific Area of Cultural Competency
A head of school should be able to oversee the development and evolution of policies and procedures to ensure equitable and inclusive working and learning environments for all members of the school community.

Knowledge related to this area:	*Skills/Abilities related to this area:*
• Current policies and practices may not be designed to be inclusive of current and future members. • Past practices may favor majority-group members at the expense of others. • More equitable and inclusive policies need accountability to be effective.	• Skills in critical analysis of policies and procedures to examine impact on all affected populations • Abilities to discuss inequitable policy impacts with key decision-makers and effectively lead the change process • Skills in building accountability into policy-change development
Knowledge and Experience Questions Institutional policies and procedures designed to ensure equity and inclusion can become out-of-date and ineffective. From your point of view, how and why does this happen? What are the challenges to identifying this? What are the issues involved in remedying it? What makes you an effective leader in this area? Please provide two examples of your leadership in this area.	*Skills and Experience Questions* Please provide at least two examples of your involvement in updating policies and procedures to increase equity and inclusion. What were the expected and unexpected challenges involved? What was your leadership role in dealing with these challenges? In each case, how would you assess the success of the change process? What skills would you bring to our school on the basis of these experiences?
Components we want to find in a "good" answer: • Demonstrated understanding that evolving populations and educational needs drive this change process • Awareness of how those benefiting from current policies may resist change • Acknowledging the difficulties involved in making needed changes	*Components we want to find in a "good" answer:* • Two distinct examples • Going beyond obvious challenges to identify unexpected ones • Candidate can articulate the leadership role the individual played in each case • Choice of appropriate evaluation methods to measure success

The template in Table 3 is designed to provide a best practices setup for documentation during the interview process. Using this template, you place all questions, including those related to culturally competent leadership, on a single page. This page also records (1) the knowledge and skills you seek by asking the question and (2) the attributes of a good answer. There is sufficient space for focused note-taking.

Perhaps most important, the rubric for evaluation is based on evidence presented in the candidate's answer. Was there very strong evidence, strong evidence, some evidence, little evidence, or no evidence of the knowledge and skills you sought? This focused evaluation approach, when taken into the post-interview discussion, means that each interviewer can be clear about what was heard and how it connects to the knowledge and skills the question was designed to bring forward.

An additional benefit of this kind of focused documentation and evaluation format is that it provides a clear paper trail for others to review as the hiring process proceeds. Table 3 illustrates this format.

Throughout this evaluation process, remember that a culturally competent school head will not have, and will not claim to have, all the answers. Rather, the head will know when questions need to be asked, when new stakeholders need to be consulted, and when what looks like an isolated problem is actually a systemic issue that needs to be recognized and addressed. The head will also know when problem-solving and decision-making processes need to be revamped to include the voices of new stakeholders so you can build a stronger, more equitable, and inclusive school community. A culturally competent school head will help your school survive and thrive in the 21st century.

1. Commit to understanding the difference between the candidate who talks a good game and the one who has the necessary skills and abilities to act on the complex cultural issues in education.

2. Have your search committee engage in critical thinking and active discussion about what a culturally competent head will bring to your school. This will result in a shared vision of pertinent knowledge, skills, and experience.

3. Focus on writing questions that provide candidates with clear

Table 3: Question Evaluation Template Example for a Head of School

Question #_____

Please provide at least two examples of your involvement in updating policies and procedures to increase equity and inclusion. What were the expected and unexpected challenges involved? What was your leadership role in dealing with these challenges? In each case, how would you assess the success of the change process? What skills would you bring to the school based on these experiences?

Skills/Knowledge related to this area

- Skills in critical analysis of policies and procedures to examine impact on all affected populations
- Abilities to discuss inequitable policy impacts with key decision-makers and to effectively lead the change process
- Skills in building accountability into the policy change development

Components in a "good" answer

- Two distinct examples
- Going beyond obvious challenges to identify unexpected ones
- Candidate can articulate the leadership role played in each case
- Choice of appropriate evaluation methods to measure success

---

INTERVIEW NOTES CAN GO HERE

- ☐ **Very strong evidence** skills/ knowledge are present

- ☐ **Strong evidence** skills/ knowledge are present

- ☐ **Some evidence** skills/ knowledge are present

- ☐ **Very little evidence** skills/ knowledge are present

- ☐ **No evidence** skills/ knowledge are present

opportunities to explain their experience in areas related to cultural competence.

4. Consider providing each candidate with the interview questions at least 30 minutes before the interview to cut down on anxiety and make the discussion more productive.

5. Identify the components of a good answer, recognizing that often this will prompt your search committee to refine the original question.

6. Realize that even when you ask effective questions, you can still sabotage the interview process and an outstanding candidate with poor documentation and unclear evaluation criteria.

Closing the Deal

15

Making the Choice

By Jane Armstrong

After the finalist visits wrap up, the search committee must reach consensus about the individuals who will best serve the identified needs of the school as a whole.

Your search committee and board have been preparing for months for this moment. Typically, it's been the search committee's job to sift through input and information; evaluate its own experiences and observations of the candidates; and, as a committee, choose a single candidate to recommend to the board.

Then the board votes on the search committee's recommendation, as it is ultimately the board's responsibility to hire the head of school.

Your search committee members must be brave and focused, bearing their responsibility to the entire school community with strong shoulders and wise heads. These individuals have been immersed in this process, calibrating candidates first on paper and next in person, shepherding candidates through finalist visits, and—especially important—immersing themselves in understanding the candidates' track records through intensive reference checking. The search committee has been privy to confidential information, much of which cannot be widely shared. It has engaged in intense conversations about the school's most significant needs. Although members arrived at the first meeting as individuals with different ideas about what kind of person should be the next head of school, successful committees have coalesced by candidly sharing their thoughts and listening to each member's perspective. They have acknowledged that there is no "perfect" candidate and come to terms with their responsibility to choose the best candidate for the entire school: the individual who will best serve the identified, agreed-upon needs of the school as a whole.

So how is the choice made? What should inform the choice? And what happens if the choice is either not obvious or really difficult?

LAYING THE GROUNDWORK FOR THE DECISION

Before the final decision, numerous pieces should be in place to lay the foundation not only for good decision-making but also for your new head's successful tenure. Good communication—within and among the search committee, the board, the candidates, and all of the school stakeholders—is important throughout the process to manage everyone's expectations. Background and reference checks should be complete in case they uncover anything that could inform the decision.

Know where your candidates are in their thinking

If you are working with a search firm, make sure your consultant connects directly with each candidate following the campus visit. While making it clear that the search is very much in process, the consultant should ask (basically), "Would you take the job if offered?" If you are not using a search consultant, the search chair should have this conversation. The point is this: You do not want your search committee thinking hard about a candidate who, after visiting the campus, decides it is not a match.

In addition, by this point there should have been at least some preliminary discussions about compensation expectations and benefits. This conversation often takes place at the conclusion of the finalist visit, when the board chair and possibly the search chair meet with the candidate to thumbnail the general compensation package and discern whether the parties are in the same general range. This approach leads to almost complete assurance that the board will be able to reach satisfactory contract terms with whichever candidate the search committee recommends. Compensation expectations and discussions are not the work of the search committee as a whole but should be managed by board leadership and the search consultant, as appropriate.

Gather community input

Along the way, all of the stakeholders who meet with each candidate should have a mechanism to share input effectively. You should emphasize with all non-committee stakeholders that you are interested in *impressions*, not seeking a *vote*. (Read more about community feedback in Chapter 4.)

Do not allow any faculty members on the search committee to hold formal or informal faculty polls as to who is the best candidate. If the committee then chooses a different candidate, it can be very damaging to that person because any public polling result, no matter how informal, will become known. This advice is equally true for any stakeholder group.

Loop in board members who aren't on the search committee

Ideally, all board members have the opportunity to meet with finalist candidates in a formal meeting and perhaps in a more social situation during the finalist visits. Afterward, board members should be asked to complete a feedback survey, an additional step that will ensure that non-committee board members feel heard before they are asked to vote on the search committee's final recommendation. Assign each board member not on the committee to a board member who is, and ask the search committee members to meet with their assigned board members to hear their impressions.

Keep special constituents in mind

There may be a few other individuals in your school community for whom an individual conversation with the chair of the search committee or the board would be prudent and respectful. Examples might include the outgoing head of school; the CFO, if the candidates have had the opportunity to have an in-depth budget discussion with the CFO during their time on campus; and the trustee emeritus/founder/key donor who needs to be appropriately stewarded. These people should be consulted without being given the impression that their "vote" will rule the decision.

Conduct background checks

Running a full background check on each finalist candidate is an additional expense but very prudent in protecting the school. Many search consultants use a professional background-checking agency to perform these checks, which typically include a review of various records, such as criminal, academic degrees, credit, and registry of motor vehicles.

If your committee has these checks done, it is essential to get them under way as soon as a candidate accepts the invitation to be a finalist. The candidates must give permission, and because these checks may include multiple state and federal databases, they can take two to three weeks. If you do not have the report in hand when you are ready to make an offer, you must make the offer contingent on a satisfactory background check.

Conduct reference checks

Reference checking should be a multilayered process, the importance of which cannot be emphasized enough. You want to hire a *track record*, not a candidate. Think of it this way: Some individuals are skilled interviewees and superficially wonderful. They can charm and answer questions with all the right words. It is the search committee's responsibility to gain deep, informed confidence that a candidate's track record—including experiences, accomplishments, and professional relationships—demonstrates deep substance and matches the attributes the school needs. Gaining a strong understanding of how an individual has actually performed in previous positions through reference checks can be the most reliable predictor of future performance.

Some search firms do initial reference checks before they present any candidate materials to a search committee. However, because of many candidates' understandable desire for confidentiality, the school often cannot undertake complete and thorough reference checking until a candidate has accepted the invitation to be a finalist. Additionally, a candidate's campus visit may raise some issues that should be explored through reference checking, and search committee members should participate in reference calls to gain an understanding of the candidate's leadership style. The independent school world is one where you can still typically engage in thoughtful reference conversations, and so you should speak to people beyond the handful of names a candidate provides.

Reference checking must be organized and orchestrated by the search consultant or the search chair. No one should undertake a formal or informal reference call without being assigned. Questions should allow for open-ended responses rather than a simple yes or no. For example, instead of asking, "Is she an effective leader?" the caller should probe for more substantial information with questions, such as "Can you describe her strengths as a leader?" or "If you were responsible for determining how to allocate professional development funds for him, what type of program would you seek to help him continue to grow as a leader?"

Individuals on the search committee who conduct these calls should take careful notes and provide them to the rest of the search committee. If information emerges that is very sensitive and could potentially sink a candidate, the search committee member who learned it should call the search chair to discuss. The search chair should then touch base with the search consultant to determine how to proceed. If you're not working with a search consultant, the search chair will need to determine how to fully assess the uncovered information. Depending on the nature of the information, a call to the candidate or additional calls—or callbacks—to other references might be appropriate.

You do not want to count out a promising candidate without thoroughly vetting an issue. But you also don't want to ignore a red flag because you know how well-received a candidate was. Remember: Hire a successful track record, not a candidate.

MAKING THE DECISION

Although the search committee's decision-making meeting should be scheduled as soon as possible after the finalists' visits, it should occur at least 24 hours after the last one has ended. It's important to give committee members time to reflect and to make sure they're not making the decision in the temporary aura of the last finalist.

But timing is often critical, as your finalists may be involved in other searches and you may have to shift from your ideal timing (see the section "Know where your candidates are in their thinking" above). So orchestrate the process carefully to ensure that when you arrive at this point, the reference checking has been completed and you've gathered the input from members of the community. Candidates should not know specifically when the search committee will make its decision or, subsequently, when the board will meet to vote on the committee's recommendation. This information should be closely held within the committee and the board so you can work through decisions and an offer without the added pressure of decisions expected on a specific day.

The big meeting

By the time your search committee members arrive at the decision-making meeting, they should have read through all the information and input. The meeting should begin with individuals sharing any new information that has been recently received. It can be helpful to review the position statement to remind committee members that their task is to select the individual who is best aligned with the school's agreed-upon needs.

Ideally, your search committee will bring a unanimous recommendation to the board. Sometimes, though, you may not be able to reach a clear decision in your initial meeting. Perhaps your committee members realize that there is critical information they still need, or maybe they're conflicted and need to "sleep on it." Many big, important decisions deserve deep and careful thought, and people make decisions differently. This decision is too important to rush if the committee has any doubts. The key is to ensure that the critical information has been gathered and shared, and that each committee member understands the importance of listening carefully to one another and deciding in the best interest of the school as a whole.

It is worth stating at this point that, of course, no candidate is perfect. Nevertheless, if your committee believes that none of the candidates is the right one, you should not make a choice simply because everyone is expecting a decision. Your school will be far better off going back to the search, even if that means considering additional candidates or an interim head of school. Hiring the wrong head of school is just too damaging and too expensive.

There are a variety of approaches to structuring this conversation. If you're working with search consultants, having them lead this meeting can help ensure that everyone has a chance to participate fully.

You may decide to take an initial poll—either through a show of hands or on paper. If there are three or more finalists, it can be helpful to begin by asking all committee members to list on a piece of paper the name(s) of the candidate they believe should still be under consideration. This tally will often eliminate one candidate from consideration or can show that your committee already agrees about a single candidate.

If your committee seems to be deciding between two candidates, it can be helpful to discuss each candidate by going around the table and having each committee member share thoughts on the strengths and concerns about each candidate.

Some committees oppose early voting and want to discuss thoroughly the pros and cons of each finalist. Some are comfortable constructing a matrix of the noted needs and discussing how each candidate matches that need (or not). No single method or approach will lead to a better decision than another, although spending a lot of time discussing a candidate whom no one supports is simply a waste of time. Whichever initial approach you take to gather the committee members' thoughts, you should have a great deal of open (but focused) dialogue. Often the dialogue makes clear that the committee is leaning in (or has arrived at) a particular direction, or it may suggest that the committee is divided. Calling for a vote will clarify where the committee stands.

If the committee is split and further discussion does not close the gap, it can help to step away and reconvene a day later. If a majority of the committee votes in favor of a specific candidate, a decision has been reached, and ideally all members of the committee will stand behind the decision so a unanimous recommendation can be brought to the board.

When the decision is reached, a report detailing the reasons should be prepared and presented to the board as the recommendation is made. At this point, your committee members must be reminded that it's extremely important to keep confidential both the specifics of the decision and the fact that the decision has indeed been reached.

After the board ratifies the committee's recommendation, the job needs to be offered formally. Ideally, the finalist will accept the offer (with some negotiation of the contract specifics), and plans for the public announcement can be put in place. Finalists who were not chosen must be called and informed before the school makes the announcement.

Then the committee's work is done.

1. See to it that your search committee gets input from numerous stakeholders who have met with candidates before making a final decision. However, non-committee stakeholders who provide input must understand that they are giving impressions; they don't have a vote or veto power. Don't take any sort of poll, formally or informally.

2. Make sure that after each finalist visits your school, your search consultant or the head of your search committee discreetly inquires whether the candidate would accept the position if asked. Hold preliminary discussions about compensation and benefit expectations to ensure that an agreement is very likely.

3. Complete background and reference checks before making any offer.

4. Keep the specific timing of the decision confidential so your committee members don't feel pressured to announce a decision on a certain day.

5. Adjourn and meet again if your committee members need more

information or some time to "sleep on it." This decision is too important to rush.

6. Remember: If the committee believes that none of the candidates is the right one, it is better to keep searching than to make a decision just because everyone expects it.

The Legalities of Reference Checks and Other Types of Screening

By Debra P. Wilson

REFERENCE CHECKS

Once you have chosen a finalist or two, your committee will begin to check references and the candidates' background. Standard reference checks typically involve talking with three or more individuals who have worked with and know the individual well. Ideally, the references can provide more information than the basics of the individual's employment. If needed, the candidate can sign a waiver giving previous employers permission to disclose information about the candidate's time at the reference institutions.

Most reference checks are fairly standard and often include questions similar to the interview questions. In many cases, those providing references will be most comfortable with factual questions, such as providing concrete examples of leadership and other skills relevant to the position. As with the interview questions, your committee or whoever is collecting the reference information needs to avoid legally prohibited topics.

BACKGROUND CHECKS

Beyond interviews and reference checks, your school should perform whatever standard background checks are usually performed on all employees. These will often include checks of sex offender registries, standard criminal background checks for areas where the individual has lived for the last 10 to 15 years, driving records, and credit reports for those individuals who have a hand in the school's finances. If your school does check credit reports, it must follow all of the required permissions of the Fair Credit Reporting Act (FCRA). Learn more about conducting background checks and complying with the FCRA on the NAIS website.

Some schools also require either physical examinations or substance testing before an employee starts a job. Note that neither of these checks may be performed prior to a job offer. The physical examination may be done only to ensure that the individual is physically capable of performing the job with or without accommodations. Any other action taken because of a physical should be done only rarely and only after consulting with the school's legal adviser.

Many schools are tempted to try the less structured background checks available through search engines, social media, or similar online outlets. If your school conducts such searches, they should be done by only one or two people and documented to ensure that they are done consistently for all the candidates being checked. Ensure that searches do not involve methods that invade candidate privacy, such as accessing personal social media accounts in ways that are not open to the public. (For example, don't use another individual's account to gain access to the candidate's personal Facebook page.) These searches should not gather or consider information that could not be openly asked or considered under federal, state, and local laws. Your school may collect and consider only information that is relevant to the position and the anticipated requirements of this position. Learn more about online background searches on the NAIS website.

Because of the unreliable, unfiltered nature of online information, your school should strongly consider allowing candidates to refute negative information that you may find.

SCREENING FOR SEXUAL OFFENSES

Since 2011, when the story broke about Penn State assistant football coach Jerry Sandusky abusing children and the failure of school officials to report what they knew to authorities, many victims of abuse in independent schools have come forward. The cases have sharpened schools' attention and resolve to provide the safest possible environments for students. Many now take extra caution in their hiring practices and that includes hiring the head of school.

In the application process, candidates should be specifically asked about any issues related to prior criminal convictions, pending charges, disciplinary action by licensing organizations, and removal from any past positions because of allegations of misconduct or mishandling of a child abuse situation.

Your school may also wish to ask whether the candidate has been involved in handling any situations at other schools where students or alumni have reported being abused. Candidates who have dealt with these issues should be given an opportunity to provide further confidential explanations. If your school is contacting other employers about these issues, you may need to secure a waiver from the candidate to gather more information on these topics from the earlier employer.

You can also ask references questions directly related to the suitability of the individual working with students, such as these:

- Do you have any concerns about this individual working with children?
- As far as you know, have there been any allegations that this candidate has had improper conduct with children?
- As far as you know, has this individual ever been part of or overseen an investigation where a child was allegedly abused?

Although many schools may assume that an individual applying for headship is outside the scope of such actions, history has shown that this is not necessarily the case. If you do not currently undertake additional steps relating to screening for involvement in past abuse scenarios, you should strongly consider doing so.

Head off unhelpful opinions. At the finalist stage, your search committee should issue clear instructions about feedback. Discourage parents, faculty, staff, students, and trustees from indicating a *preference* for one candidate or another. That does not help you weigh their comments against your established selection criteria.

Instead, ask community members to describe each candidate's strengths and weaknesses (or areas for growth or support). This helps with effective decision-making, avoids the appearance of a popular vote, and reinforces the board's authority to make the final choice. It also reduces the chance that divisive factions will emerge in favor of one candidate or another.

Lee Quinby, Executive Director, Association of Colorado Independent Schools

Take the long view. Committees often hesitate initially on candidates with limited experience in particular areas (most often fundraising, enrollment management, or finance). We recommend that search committees "hire what you can't teach." Every committee starts the process wanting a perfect 10, but many heads who have "only" seven or eight of the 10 most desirable characteristics, and who assemble a strong admin team, turn out to be wonderfully impressive leaders.

Ted Lingenheld, Managing Partner, School Strategies and Solutions

Don't settle for the wrong person! At the outset of your search, identify some strong interim head choices to have in your pocket so you won't feel desperate. An appointment like this is too important—financially, psychologically, emotionally, and culturally—to botch.

Rhonda Durham, Executive Director, Independent Schools Association of the Southwest

16

Setting Compensation and Building the Contract

By Debra P. Wilson

■ You can lessen legal risk and increase the prospect of a good relationship with your new head by following a carefully conceived process to determine compensation and contract terms.

Schools worry quite a bit about legal vulnerability, but by the time they worry, often those vulnerabilities have already morphed into risk. Like any other entity, schools are better served by mitigating those vulnerabilities before they become risks. Many of the steps and action items you take to address the school's needs should provide clarity to help mitigate your risks as well. Previous chapters have touched on potential risks in the search and selection process. Here we will focus on the process of setting compensation and developing the contract.

SETTING REASONABLE COMPENSATION

The board should set a compensation range early, ideally before the search has even begun. This early range determination allows the school to be clear with the candidates and sets some parameters for later negotiations, ensuring that they will be within the range appropriate for the school. Your board can deviate slightly for exceptional skills, etc., as the compensation package comes to an official vote, but identifying a compensation range early on will lay a foundation for later success. The school may choose to advertise the salary range. But any related materials should note that the final salary level will be based on a number of factors, including the candidate's relevant experience and education, and that the salary isn't final until an official offer is made and accepted.

What Does the IRS Say?

School people sometimes have a hard time talking about money. Your board does not want to unnecessarily limit itself in its hiring approach, nor does it want to spend too much. At the same time, your candidates do not want to come across as overly focused on the compensation package. The good news is that the Internal Revenue Service requires that all compensation to executives of nonprofits must be reasonable, and this requirement will add context and help your board set parameters for compensation decisions.

For the IRS, reasonableness means that the total compensation package must be reasonable relative to the size of the nonprofit, the work it does, the market that it is in, and other similar factors. This reasonable standard applies to all "disqualified people," those who have been in their positions for at least five years and influence the business practices of the nonprofit to the extent that their compensation deserves special scrutiny. Disqualified people include those within the school who have a distinct amount of say in the operations of the school (such as the head of school and often the business officer and division heads) and who have been in their positions for the past five years.

The first compensation agreement for your new head, if drafted properly, is considered exempt to some degree from what the IRS calls "intermediate sanctions." (Learn more about intermediate sanctions below.) But since the initial compensation package will be the base for the next agreement, reasonable compensation must be considered from the start.

Setting a Reasonable Range and Avoiding Penalties

Before you can agree on a reasonable salary, you must be sure that the compensation range you set before the search begins is reasonable. The range can be fairly broad, but it should reflect the school's thinking about compensation as well as defensible benchmarks. Such benchmarks may be based on your school's enrollment, budget, location, and other traits. The range within those benchmarks may reflect the school's overall budget philosophy (e.g., "Between the 50th to 75th percentiles within our benchmark groups, with potential for additional income in the event of exceptional experience or skills"). Having a range and a philosophy ensures that your school will be speaking with candidates who are truly appropriate for the school. The range will also help your school later when it must comply with tax laws that demand reasonable compensation.

If your board does not take steps to ensure the reasonableness of the compensation, the IRS can assess "intermediate sanctions," penalties for both the individual who receives excess compensation and the body that approves it. If sanctions are levied, the individual must pay back the excess compensation, plus a 25 percent penalty on the excess amount. Organizational managers, including board members, who knowingly and willfully sign off on the compensation without other reasonable cause can be liable for up to 10 percent of the excess benefit or $10,000, whichever is less.

Documenting the Decision

The standard process for setting reasonableness by IRS standards is generally not required for an initial contract. But it is a good practice for a board to have the process in place because the board will be reviewing the compensation again if the contract is extended, renewed, or amended.

To meet the IRS requirements of presumed reasonableness of the compensation, your board must, as a whole or as a committee, review the compensation data, determine the compensation, and document the decision. The IRS prefers the entire board to act on the compensation, and this is a best practice. Regardless of whether the full board or a committee makes the decision, the committee should look at data from at least three to five schools, and no voting member should have any conflicts of interest.

Here's what the documentation should include:

- Who was on the committee or board that was voting
- Confirmation that voters were asked and did not have any conflicts of interest
- Any data that were used and considered
- Notes on any discussion
- The final vote

The notes from this vote should be prepared and approved by the voting body at the next meeting or within 60 days, whichever is later.

How a Consultant Could Help

The IRS permits use of a compensation or other consultant to provide professional advice on reasonable compensation. Consultants generally create a list of like organizations and then either contact the organizations directly or work from their 990 forms to gather the compensation information. The consultant then walks your board or a committee through all the data and provides a letter or other form of certification as to the reasonableness of the compensation package the board agreed to. As long as the reliance on this third-party professional is reasonable, the IRS will generally agree that the board did not willfully and knowingly approve excess compensation.

PUTTING TOGETHER THE PACKAGE

Once your search committee and board have chosen your final candidate, the board will appoint a committee to move forward with negotiating the final agreement with the new head of school. This group might be the executive committee, an existing compensation committee, or the search committee itself. The makeup of the committee does not matter all that much, as long as it is small enough to move quickly to review terms, offers, and counteroffers. The committee may decide to work through the school's attorney or through one-on-one conversations with the candidate. The board vote authorizing this committee to move forward with the negotiation should be clear about the compensation parameters within which the committee can negotiate.

Setting the Right Tone

The tone of these exchanges is extremely important for building initial trust between your board and the incoming head of school. Both parties want to come to a fair compensation package and overall agreement without ruining that relationship from the beginning.

If your board lacks the expertise to carry out these negotiations, it's vital to work with an experienced attorney or other adviser who understands the importance of preserving the future relationship as well as the school's finances. The incoming head should also hire an attorney to review the agreement. This ensures that the head understands the terms and has a knowledgeable person reviewing the agreement on the head's behalf.

Having both parties represented can move the conversation from the parties to the attorneys, which can help defuse any potential conflict between the board and the head of school.

Deciding Who Should Represent Your School

Your board should consider carefully whether to use the school's regular legal counsel in the compensation negotiations. If the conversations become uncomfortable, the new head of school might be less inclined to use this lawyer in the future, and the school will lose that institutional memory. In addition, not all school attorneys are well-versed in negotiating contracts for and with the head of school.

That said, there is nothing that would automatically disqualify your board from using the regular school attorney. The important thing is that the board believes that the attorney can reasonably represent the board while ensuring that the tone of the exchanges is respectful and preserves the necessary early trust.

What a Compensation Package Could Include

The compensation range you set should give the committee a fair amount of flexibility. Designing a package with the needs of the new head of school in mind can provide much goodwill with the head and family members. Through the latter part of the search process, you will likely gain some insight into the kinds of compensation the finalist candidates are seeking. If you are using a search consultant, the consultant can begin having those conversations at the finalist stage.

The following elements are all potential compensation items. The list is by no means exclusive. While many of these items have tax benefits, such as deferring taxation on income, many do not. Although it would seem to be less complex to gross up the salary for items such as child care or tuition assistance for a spouse, having these items as separate benefits keeps them as temporary benefits in the compensation structure. Lowering salary levels is much more difficult than sunsetting benefits that have a natural endpoint. Compensation for temporary items can help address the head of school's current life needs while not building the temporary benefits into the actual salary.

- **Salary and deferred compensation**
  - Annual base salary
  - Cash bonus
  - Deferred compensation funded by your school
    1. Key executive insurance policy (school as beneficiary)
    2. Rabbi trust (irrevocable trust usually set up by contract)

3. Separate investment

4. 403(b) (a standard retirement plan, similar to a 401(k) plan)

5. 457(b) (an additional tax-deferred retirement plan)

6. 457(f) (a contractual plan typically used to ensure that the employee stays for a specified time period or until certain goals are met)

7. Deferred cash payments

8. Any other type of deferred compensation

9. Contributions to standard benefits (usually standard for most school employees; consider the amount the school actually pays on behalf of the disqualified person)

- **Standard benefits that may or may not be altered for the head of school**
  - Disability insurance
  - Life insurance
  - Medical insurance
  - Dental insurance
  - Liability insurance
  - Flexible benefits
  - Retirement plan contributions
  - Any other standard benefits contributions

- **Other compensation.** These benefits are generally not provided to employees besides the head of school and, occasionally, other upper-level administrators.
  - Moving expenses
  - Attorney's fees for reviewing the agreement
  - Forgone interest on loans
  - Forgiven loan principal
  - Education assistance plan
  - Tuition remission
  - Tuition benefit (beyond standard remission and including other kinds of tuition or other school-related benefits)
  - Additional insurance
  - Spouse travel allowance or payments
  - Child care allowance (to cover costs of child care during travel to school events)

- Campus housing
- Off-campus housing
- Parking or transit passes
- Auto allowance
- Nonincidental personal use of a school vehicle
- Club membership or dues
- Professional membership organization dues
- Sabbatical opportunities (cashed out instead of taken)
- Vacation (cashed out instead of taken)
- Sick leave (cashed out instead of taken)
- Financial planning consulting
- Executive coaching for a period of time
- Special funds for additional professional development early in a head of school's tenure

USING A TERM SHEET TO SMOOTH CONTRACT NEGOTIATIONS

The first round of negotiations is generally not a full contract but rather a key term sheet, which is a nonbinding agreement with basic terms you can use as a template for the contract. Having the term sheet allows the parties to negotiate through standard terms and specific benefits, such as the ones in the list above, and key terms of the agreement. The board committee usually puts the initial term sheet together, with the help of legal counsel, for the nominee's review and consideration. The following terms are ones your committee should be particularly aware of and the parties should discuss carefully.

- **Renewal or extension terms.** This is usually the date by which the parties will discuss the renewal, extension, or nonrenewal of the employment agreement. This term usually provides for this determination a year before the contract will end, although it may be slightly less. A one-year notice gives the head of school ample time to seek new employment if the board doesn't wish to renew the agreement, and it provides the school a year to find and sign the next head of school.

- **Termination without cause terms.** This term is a pre-negotiated severance amount in the event that the board decides to terminate the agreement without cause. This term can be one of the most difficult

■ Resources

"Compensation Issues for Heads of School": https://www.nais.org/articles/pages/compensation-issues-for-school-heads/

"An Introduction to Intermediate Sanctions" (IRS, complete with checklists): https://www.irs.gov/pub/irs-tege/eotopich02.pdf

"NAIS Guide to Executive Contracts": http://www.nais.org/Articles/Pages/Member/Executive-Contracts.aspx

NAIS Independent School Guide to Hiring: http://www.nais.org/Articles/Pages/Independent-School-Hiring-Guide.aspx

to negotiate for a head of school position because, with head of school searches, timing is everything.

For example, if the board terminates an agreement in October, it might not be reasonable to expect the head of school to find comparable new employment until July 1 of the following year at the earliest. The contract should address this issue. Some schools specify that the head of school will continue to receive a salary; the school will pay for COBRA benefits for one year after termination; and the head of school has an obligation to mitigate the expenses of the school by continuing to look for employment to offset the payment amounts.

Although this is not an approach seen in many industries, committees should understand that the school employment cycle, particularly for heads of school, is highly regimented, leaving few opportunities in the off season.

- **Resignation.** This term usually includes the expected amount of notice the head of school should give the board before leaving. If the head of school is receiving a 457(f) "golden handcuffs" plan, the amount is usually forfeited if the individual resigns before the end of the agreement. This term may or may not include a provision that addresses the situation if the head is a finalist in another search.

- **Work or other professional obligations outside of school.** This covers whether the new head of school may consult or provide other services during personal time. It is better to address this issue up front to ensure that both parties understand the parameters. Some schools allow this work, some do not, and still others require preauthorization from the board chair.

- **Noncompete clauses.** Although the enforceability of these clauses can vary greatly in different states, more schools have been considering them in recent years.

The term sheet provides a clean mechanism for the parties to see the key terms that are most important to the parties outside of the more involved legal language of a built-out contract. Although schools can certainly move directly to the contract phase, many schools and businesses have found pre-negotiating the terms helps decrease the time spent on the actual agreement. See a sample term sheet in Appendix F.

Once the parties have agreed to the key terms, legal counsel should document them in an agreement that takes into account both the terms and the state and federal laws that may apply. The head of school's attorney will also review the agreement and work out the final language. Although there may still be a bit of back-and-forth through the actual contract process, the term sheet should address most of the key terms, and the contract process itself should contain very few surprises as a rule.

A GOOD PROCESS MITIGATES RISK

Your school's overall search process should address potential legal vulnerabilities. The steps you take to mitigate risk can also help strengthen the committee's focus and knowledge of the candidates as well as the board's position on important topics, such as compensation and the terms required for the parties to move ahead with a successful relationship.

1. Set the compensation range early in your process, ideally before you begin your search.
2. Think carefully about your compensation package and the many different kinds of compensation available.

3. Negotiate with a small committee of the board to ensure that negotiations can move quickly.

4. Keep the tone of negotiations respectful to build the early trust needed for this relationship to flourish. Use trusted and knowledgeable counselors or advisers as needed.

5. Use a term sheet to narrow down the most important compensation and contractual aspects of the final contract.

6. Use legal counsel for both sides to draft and review the term sheet and contract as necessary.

SECTION F

Saying Goodbye and Hello

17

Smoothing the Transition

By Christopher B. Arnold, Jerry Larson, and Agnes Underwood

> ◼ You must orchestrate the transition from old to new with the same care and attention to detail that you devoted to the search itself.

At last your board of trustees has appointed your new head of school. Now the trustees must be fully committed to leading volunteers, staff, and faculty through a thoughtful and well-planned transition period. The months between the announcement and the end of the first year of service are crucial to ensuring a long and successful tenure for your new head.

The transition timetable in Appendix G offers an abbreviated to-do list for the months ahead. As it makes clear, to get the new era off to a good start, the school's leaders must announce the new head's arrival with flair, handle the former head's departure with grace, attend to the thousand details of the transition and orientation, and set goals with support systems in place that will give the new head a firm direction.

MAKING THE ANNOUNCEMENT

The transition to new leadership begins in earnest with the announcement process. At this point your primary goal is to allow your school and the broader community to learn more about the newly appointed head. But the announcement also presents a wealth of opportunities to acquaint others with your school's mission and programs and to welcome everyone to campus. To take full advantage of the opportunities this change presents, you should structure and plan this phase with great care.

But first things first. Before you announce the appointment, you must have in hand a guaranteed commitment from the candidate. This can be a signed letter of intent, a signed contract, or both. Understandably, the candidate may want a personal attorney to review the employment contract—a process that may take some time. For this reason, best practices suggest that, in most cases, you should execute a letter of intent for the new head's signature so that you can begin the announcement process promptly. (Read more about contracts in Chapter 16.)

Once the commitment is sealed, the staff should develop a clear communication plan that outlines the order and methods of announcing the appointment. You can get the word out in a number of different ways in the following approximate order. By crafting your wording carefully, you can reuse the information in a variety of different formats.

- **Email and social media.** To get the word out quickly, most schools send a simple announcement to constituents on their email distribution lists and post the announcement on their website and to their social media followers. Later you may send a more formal announcement by mail, as suggested below. You might also consider a video announcement that includes a brief introductory statement from your new head, which you can post to the various social media platforms where the school has a presence.

- **Mail.** Follow up your email message with a formal announcement containing descriptive information about the candidate's experience, qualifications, family, and personal interests. Include a photograph if possible, along with a quote from the head-elect. The announcement, often written over the signature of the search chair or board chair, should be warm and welcoming in tone (see Appendix H). Fewer schools are mailing formal announcements, but they are still an effective way to connect with your most loyal constituents. Not everyone on your postal mailing lists follows you on social media or is on your email list, and even those who are may not actually read such communications.

- **Via the media and other groups.** Gather lists of contacts beyond the school community who should receive the announcement, possibly in the form of a news release. This list should include newspapers and other local media outlets in addition to such groups as all NAIS schools, other regional and national associations, and local colleges and universities. Don't forget to schedule an article in your own school magazine when appropriate—perhaps you'll publish an initial announcement and follow up with a full profile.

- **Phone calls.** The search chair and other appointed trustees can make personal calls about the appointee to several important people in the community, such as local officials, past trustees, and significant donors. The personal communication of this important information makes people feel engaged and close to the school. You may also consider a meeting with these people or perhaps a special visit when the head-elect is going to be on campus.

- **In-person events.** Begin immediately to plan a welcoming gathering (usually called a convocation or installation) for the new head in the fall. This is one of the most significant public relations opportunities during the transition period. Plan to include opportunities for the new head and the board chair to speak briefly, and, if possible, arrange for a prominent speaker. Like many schools, you may also want to have welcoming presentations from students, faculty, parents, and alumni. Invite the entire school community and all local media outlets as well as prominent citizens and friends of the school. Then have a celebratory reception following the program. Given the importance of continually cultivating alumni, parents, and friends, consider regional events in the first year as another way for the head to get to know the school community.

Additionally, consider ways to introduce the new head to the neighborhood and local officials with whom the school interacts. You can do this through a reception or meeting in the fall, soon after the head arrives. It's never too soon to build good relationships with your neighbors and city and town officials.

BOARD RESPONSIBILITIES

Even if you have a transition committee in place (see Chapter 18), during the transition period the entire board must help perform a number of high-level duties. These include preparing the community for change, saying farewell to the former head, welcoming and supporting the head-elect and family, and setting appropriate goals and expectations for the first few years of new leadership.

Change is difficult for everyone everywhere, but this seems especially so in some school cultures. Board members should see to it that there is a good process in place for the transition and be fully aware of their role in it as spokespersons for both the old and the new. Board members must attend all transition events and lend their support and experience as needed. There should also be a clear board leadership succession process in place, ideally with the next chair coming from the ranks of the search committee.

Saying goodbye to the former head

Making plans to recognize and send off the departing head is an important part of every transition. An essential first step: The board chair, in particular, must ensure that the current head remains fully in charge until the successor takes office, usually on July 1. The chair should make this clear—throughout the search and after the selection of the new head—in conversations with constituent groups as well as in written communications from the board. In the meantime, the chairs of both the board and the search committee should encourage the head and head-elect to talk about the most amiable and effective ways to transfer leadership.

When it comes to recognizing and honoring the departing head, you can follow any of several available models, from modest and informal to large and grand. Base the scope of your celebrations on criteria such as these:

- The longevity and contributions of the head to the school community
- School traditions
- How comfortable the head is in the spotlight

A fitting farewell might be a convocation that includes students, parents, faculty, alumni, and trustees. In addition to providing an appropriate speaker, each constituency could present a small token of thanks to the departing head. The event could be followed by a reception or a special trustee dinner. Other possibilities include recognition of the departing head at graduation or a series of smaller events given by each of the constituencies noted above.

If the departing head is leaving at the board's request or has had a short tenure, it is still very important for the school to say thank you in a formal and graceful way. You could do this with a short tribute—if not at a special event, then as part of a regularly scheduled end-of-school event or at a board meeting.

Whatever you decide, remember that honoring a long-term head presents yet another opportunity to talk to the broader community about your school's accomplishments. Local newspapers and community publications may be good vehicles for articles (as well as your alumni magazine).

Saying hello to the new head

As the school welcomes the new head, the board must demonstrate its appreciation and support in both tangible and intangible ways. The board and the new head should work to develop an effective and strong partnership from the beginning to avoid miscommunication and misunderstandings down the road. It is your board's job to introduce the head to your community by planning social events with various constituencies, from students and parents to major donors and community leaders.

And at all times in public, all volunteer leaders, including all members of the board and search committee, must speak positively of your new head. If anyone has suggestions for improvements in the head's performance, he or she should work through appropriate evaluation channels or the board chair. This is often the most critical aspect of a head of school transition and the one most frequently overlooked by the board.

Setting goals

When getting down to business before the head begins on July 1, the board (often a small committee appointed by the chair) and board chair should work closely with the head-elect to develop goals and expectations for—at the very least—the first year. Many transition plans set goals for 18 months to two years, which reflects a greater sense of reality about how long the full transition period can take. This work and other transition planning often begin in early spring before the head is to take office. You should also mutually agree on a clear evaluation structure and feedback plan. This is a critical part of the transition. Goals and expectations should be both realistic and clearly defined and should be based on institutional planning. It is wise to keep these early goals small in number as well as simple and straightforward. For example, one might be "Get to know the school community and its constituencies by meeting with faculty, students, parents, and alumni." Then you might follow a general goal like this with simple action steps. Developing strong head-board relationships and building trust are essential to a new leader's success.

Once the goals are established, publicize the general agenda the board has set for the new head so that the school community knows what to expect and what *not* to expect (see Appendix I). If the school is planning any major decisions for which the head-elect is *not* responsible, the board should be accountable and make the community aware of this fact. That first year sets the tone for head-board relationships. The board's support, encouragement, and engagement are crucial to that process.

One of the most recent and important additions for heads in transition is the use of an executive coach for the first year or two of leadership. Although this has been a long-term practice in corporations and higher education, it is a fairly new concept in independent schools. Executive coaching differs from mentoring because executive coaches must complete a formal, recognized coach training that prepares them in this discipline. The combination of school leadership experience and coaching expertise can significantly help leaders grow, improve, and succeed. A successful program usually consists of both in-person visits and regular telephone or Skype sessions meant to build a strong and collaborative relationship between coach and head. Executive coaching has proved to be very helpful to both new and experienced heads and has led to more successful transitions and outcomes.

As mentioned above, the board and the new head need to develop a strong relationship to ensure an effective partnership. It is not too early to think about creating a subcommittee of the board to provide a mechanism for the head to

■ The Board Chair's Special Responsibilities

As the individual most responsible for nurturing a positive, productive partnership with the new head, the board chair must commit considerable time and energy to these important tasks:

- Work with the full board to develop a transition plan

- Provide the chief financial officer and all trustees with the details of the new head's compensation package

- Help the new head understand the subtleties of the dynamics within the school's administrative team and the board

- Set an appropriate time and process for the head's first evaluation— with a commitment to conduct subsequent yearly evaluations

- Sign up—with the new head—for relevant NAIS professional development opportunities related to good governance

- Engage in regular, frequent, and candid conversation with the new head, whether a seasoned pro or a rookie, especially over the course of the first year seek input, advice, and support, as well as assessment. We see schools engaging an executive coach or supporting a peer discussion group as a way to support the head of school. It is a good reminder that, for the most part, every relationship the head has within the school community is multidimensional. So relationships are more complex, and it may be difficult for the head to develop truly authentic friendships. It is also important for the board to pay attention to the head's family and how they are adapting to their new situation.

OTHER WAYS TO ORIENT THE NEW HEAD OF SCHOOL

Beyond the helpful guidance of a transition committee (see Chapter 18), your school should make the best possible use of the several months it will have to prepare your new head for the July 1 start. Here are some ideas:

- A major help for a first-time head is NAIS's Institute for New Heads.
- If you're working with a search firm, don't take for granted that your consultants' work is finished, especially if you arranged for some transition services as part of your agreement.
  - Ask for help developing a specific transition plan for your school.
  - Expect your consultants to provide information they have gleaned about special needs of the head-elect's family.
  - Request examples of various communications, such as announcements and press releases, which you can use as models or idea-starters for telling the community about your head.
  - Take full advantage of your consultants' expertise—they may well be experienced former school heads—when you have questions about the transition and governance.
- Put the head-elect on the mailing list and email distribution list for all school publications and announcements.
- Provide any information on school operations that you didn't already include in the information packets for semifinalist and finalist candidates. Board meeting notes are particularly helpful, as is information on faculty and staff (along with photos).
- Ask your current head to prepare a list of any special things that may have become expected traditions in the minds of the school community. For example, often there is an opening faculty party of some kind with welcoming traditions or special recognition of long-serving faculty.

PREPARATION PAYS OFF

Only with time will the new head truly learn the culture of your school. But you can shorten that time by helping the individual understand the nuances of your school community as thoroughly as possible.

After the school announces its decision, the process by which the search committee converts into the transition committee and welcomes the head (and family) makes an indelible impression—good or bad. That is why you must orchestrate the transition with the same care and attention to detail you devoted to the search itself.

1. Establish a transition plan with a timeline and a dedicated transition committee.

2. Be strategic about your communications plan. Recognize that this is an opportunity to educate the wider community about your school's mission, philosophy, values, and educational outcomes.

3. Don't forget to celebrate and honor your departing head; this signals how the school values leadership.

4. Have a board leadership succession plan in place.

5. Consider an executive coach for your new head of school. Don't forget to support the head's family.

6. Set goals. The board chair and selected trustees (perhaps called a head's assessment and support committee), in partnership with the new head, should establish clear goals and measurable objectives and should put in place regular feedback routines for the first year and beyond.

7. Communicate. Be very strategic with all your communication, not only about the transition but also with your head of school. Establish the routine early and be consistent.

8. Be supportive. Encourage the new head to sign up for relevant NAIS professional development opportunities.

Fight feelings of isolation with an executive coach. A wise board includes executive coaching in the head's compensation package. Like corporate leaders and great athletes, heads can find coaching to be a healthy part of their personal and professional development. It can provide the support needed to meet the demands of leading a school and achieving the goals the board sets.

George Conway, President, Independent Educational Services (IES)

Remember that selecting the head-elect is just the first hurdle. Ensure a successful transition by establishing a healthy, trusting, supportive relationship between the board chair and the new head so that the bumps in the road can be experienced with as little upset as possible.

Jean Lamont, Partner, Educators' Collaborative

18

The Transition Committee

By Thomas J. Banks and Kendall R. Cameron

■ A well-established transition committee provides an ideal opportunity for planning, orientation, and reflection.

As your search committee celebrates a successful hire, your transition committee's work is only beginning. To help ensure a smooth head of school transition, the board should form an ad hoc transition committee to serve from the moment of the announcement through the first year of the new head's tenure. The makeup and size of the committee will depend on your school's needs (see the section on size and constituent makeup below). But the two overarching goals are the same: (1) to guarantee that the outgoing head exits with dignity and grace and (2) to provide the incoming head with support to help ensure success.

Of course, there are several other important aspects to your transition committee's work. These include providing your incoming head with a first opportunity to exercise leadership and starting to build the relationship between the new head and board chair—arguably the most important relationship in an independent school. Your transition committee must attend to tasks both large and small, from planning and implementing the various events introducing the new head to different constituencies, to making sure the new stationery and business cards have been ordered so they're available when the head arrives. (See the list of possible tasks for the transition committee later in this chapter.)

CLARIFYING ROLES

When forming the transition committee, your board chair needs to clearly define the varying roles of the transition committee and the board. Who will write the charge to the new head of school? Who will work with the new head on finalizing goals? Who will work with the school's marketing and communications office on the communication plan around head of school succession? Who will track and approve transition spending to ensure that the transition remains on budget?

These are all questions that your board chair should discuss with the transition committee (or its chair) before the transition work begins. Confusion over who is responsible for the important tasks of the transition can cause frustration, damage the early relationship between your trustees and the incoming head, and undermine your new head's success. If not on the transition com-

■ Possible Tasks for the Transition Committee

The transition committee and the board should never cross the line into school operations. Nevertheless, once the transition committee establishes a working relationship with your new leader, the individual can benefit from the committee's knowledge and support. The following list shows how the committee, working in conjunction with the staff, can prepare the way for both the head and the school.

- Schedule transition visits, if possible and appropriate, and ensure that your new head has whatever is needed for these to be successful.
- Introduce your new head to the community.
- Connect your outgoing head of school with your incoming head for semi-regular conversations around staffing and personnel matters, important community relations, ongoing or pending legal matters, board personnel and structure, or any other topics they should discuss.
- Help your new head plan the transition for family members, including locating housing, securing a spouse's employment, and getting school-age children settled.
- Help the family find a faith community, if this is important to them.
- Plan and implement all communication around the transition.
- Plan and implement celebrations for your outgoing head of school.
- Plan and implement your welcome and, if institutionally traditional, installation events for your new head of school.

mittee, your board chair should maintain regularly scheduled communication with the transition committee so that all trustees are fully aware of all transition activities.

COMMUNICATION OPPORTUNITIES

Communication is vital and should be strategically leveraged to engage all of your school's stakeholders during the transition. A carefully crafted communication plan begins long before the transition stage. The plan includes the announcement that the current head is leaving as well as the plan and timeline

- Assist your head of school and family with all moving logistics.
- Orient your new head and family to the school's local community.
- Familiarize your new head with the school's important traditions.
- Ensure that your new head has everything needed in the office (furniture, lighting, etc.).
- Work with your new head on first-year goals.
- Orient your new head to important trustee-level documents. (See the documents list in the Transition Timeline and Activities section.)
- Anticipate potentially challenging relationships or situations— including institutional wounds that your new head might have a fresh start in healing—and alert your new head about them.
- Identify calendar items and events that your new head should attend and ensure that they are on the head's personal calendar. Follow up to ensure your new head is prepared and properly supported to play a role in these events.
- Identify calendar items and events that would be appropriate for your new head's spouse or partner to attend, and ensure that these are communicated.
- Check in consistently throughout the first year to ensure that your new head has everything needed to be successful.

your board has put into place for the search. The communications should involve written statements as well as events where the new head may be present. They should also be sure to target all your school's important constituencies: faculty, alumni, parents, students, members of the local community, education colleagues in the local and broader community, board members, and other friends of the school.

There are many possible communication opportunities during the transition period:

- An invitation to the celebration/farewell event for your outgoing head
- The introduction of the transition committee to all your school constituencies
- Occasional updates from the transition committee about its work with your new head and family
- A letter of introduction from your new head of school to families who have enrolled or who are considering enrolling
- Invitations to welcome events introducing your new head and family to the community
- Videos introducing your new head to the community
- Social media posts, including pictures of your new head of school interacting with various school constituents
- Your head of school's welcome message on the school's website

That said, the board chair and vice chair should convey to your new head the general purpose and direction of the transition committee as it is being formed. Ideally, the transition committee allows everyone to practice their new relationships in a microcosm of what will become the board-head relationship.

THE TRANSITION COMMITTEE'S SIZE
AND CONSTITUENT MAKEUP

Your search committee and your transition committee have different objectives, which are reflected in the composition and size of the groups. When building a search committee, your school may well see constituent group representation as a primary goal. The need to include a wide variety of perspectives and the work itself dictate the group's framework, which will usually result in a large search committee.

By contrast, your transition committee's work calls for a smaller forum with a larger set of objectives. Your transition committee will generally have to function nimbly in many topic areas, and ideally it will facilitate a mentoring relationship between members of the committee and your new head. More specifically, your new head needs to have a comfortable arena (in addition to the head-chair relationship) to ask questions on potentially sensitive topics and to test the cultural waters within a confidential, honest, and supportive environment. A small committee that is able to discuss, reflect, and reach consensus quickly is often advantageous.

One model is a team of four or five. These should include the two essential members: your board chair and your new head of school. The transition committee opportunity is the ideal forum for the development of this vital working relationship. (If your next board chair is already identified, the incoming board chair should also be part of the transition team.)

The next member of the transition committee is ideally a representative of your school's current senior leadership team who can also take on the administrative role of onboarding the new head and family. This person can provide the committee with insider institutional perspective. If the search committee has used a search liaison throughout the process, that person is uniquely poised to play this role, since it provides continuity through the search, the selection, and the head's transition.

The final member should be another board member, ideally within the executive committee, to provide an additional board perspective.

Some schools opt for a larger transition committee that represents more constituencies. These could include a student, an alumna or alumnus, a faculty member, and sometimes a parent. Your school culture and its circumstances at the time of hire will factor into the size and makeup of the transition committee.

■ Suggested Transition Team Membership

- Board chair for the coming academic year (and the next board chair, if identified)
- Incoming head of school
- Senior leadership team member (preferably the search liaison, described in Chapter 3)
- Additional board member—vice chair or member of the executive committee

Regardless of the committee size, your incoming head of school should be the primary driver of all discussion agendas.

THE TRANSITION TIMELINE AND ACTIVITIES

How long the transition period lasts is a matter of debate, but it's important to come to an agreement within your school so you can determine the transition committee's scope.

Some argue that the transition is only in effect until the head arrives. Others see it as a period of about 18 months—from time of hire until the conclusion of the new head's first year. Still others see it as a full two years from the time of hire—enough for the new head to both see and affect all school customs. In reality, most agree that the full transition into school life takes three years, but the question for your transition committee to decide is this: How much of that should be under careful management?

The default for a planned transition time period is from date of the contract agreement until the end of your new head's first school year. How active and involved the transition committee gets will depend on what your new head wants and needs, but extending the transition time to the end of the school year ensures that there is support available through the first cycle.

The importance of an early start

The transition committee's start, timing, and pace can be determined in a quick conversation between your new head and board leadership. The typical July 1 start date is an important benchmark for the transition committee, and a timeline can be designed working backward from there.

Determining many of your committee's goals and objectives requires taking the actual start date into consideration. It takes months of preparation to deliver a smooth entry on July 1, and starting at the beginning of the calendar year gives you a full six months prior to the start date—an ideal amount of time. If your head is hired at a later date, you can develop the committee structure in advance of the time when the head can get involved. However, we recommend against beginning the actual committee work before the new head can participate.

By starting early, you will have a more relaxed load of necessary agenda items. You'll also have more opportunity to discuss, listen, and reflect on the perspective of all members on the transition committee and more time to allow the working relationships to develop. As the July 1 start date looms closer, more operations-related topics must be covered, and you should set appropriate boundaries to be sure that trustees do not overstep. An early start gives you the luxury of time to discuss long-term objectives, set goals, and establish expected protocols of communication.

Topics for discussion

Here are some suggested topics at the early stages of your transition committee's work:

- Determination of a working timeline, frequency of meetings, goals, and agenda development responsibilities
- Review of the board members' biographies and any long-term goals with respect to the development of board membership
- Sharing of historically successful and unsuccessful past practices regarding the operation of the school
- Prior strategic plan guidelines and the timeline for any future strategic planning processes
- Current staffing issues and your new head's involvement in hiring for the following academic year
- Financial status of the school and complete disclosure of challenges

Questions for your new head to ask

Tying entry to the understanding of school culture is important. The new head's time with the relatively small transition committee is an opportunity to explore in more depth the committee members' thoughts and ideas. Additionally, the committee can direct the new head on avenues to explore in conversations with board members who are not on the transition committee.

Potential questions your new head can ask members of the transition team, as well as members of the board during individual interviews, include these:

- What do you believe are the school's core values?
- What are the school's core challenges?
- What are your dreams and hopes for the school this year, next year, and in the next five years?
- What do you think I should know about the school that I might not already know?
- What successful changes have you observed at the school, and why do you think they were successful?

- What unsuccessful changes have you observed at the school, and why do you think they failed?

Relevant documents

In addition to hearing opinions through conversation, your transition committee can use several documents and resources:

- Employee handbook
- Parent handbook
- Student handbook
- School bylaws
- Accreditation report
- Board minutes
- Admission materials, including statistics
- Strategic plan
- Campus master plan
- Development statistics from the previous three to five years
- 990 federal reports, budgets, and audits
- Relevant historical data from NAIS's online platform, Data and Analysis for School Leadership (DASL)

More operational, nonfiduciary documents—such as a curriculum guide, college counseling information, or emergency response system—can be handled by the head in transition meetings with the administrative team, preferably through the search liaison.

TRANSITION VISITS

If both your incoming and outgoing heads agree, it is ideal to have one or two transition visits in the months leading up to the July 1 start. For these visits to be productive, it is essential for your new and departing heads to be seen as allies. Your departing head should be gracious in sharing the campus, and your head-elect should remain a guest until the term of employment begins. The transition committee can determine the agenda for these visits in advance, but the occasions should generally be seen as "summit meetings" between the transitioning heads.

The responsibility for planning and stewarding each visit rests with the transition committee, not the head of school, so that the theme of developing new working relationships is maintained. The two heads will also have their own relationship as predecessor and successor, so it is important for that dynamic to develop in a healthy way. If possible, they should meet at least at the beginning and end of each visit day.

Any visit to campus by your new head of school should be introductory in nature, with events planned to introduce the new head to the students, community, alumni, faculty, and staff, who will naturally be curious about their new leader. Providing the opportunity for different constituents to become more familiar with your new head can help ease any anxieties related to the transition.

Any visit by your new head before the start date should be purposely designed so that the new head is not dealing with current operations or planning. Any involvement in decision-making or planning should be done indirectly, in collaboration with your current head or the transition committee. Your new head, the rest of the transition committee, and the outgoing head should discuss this issue early and agree on the level of the new head's involvement on specific issues, including staffing and any operational changes for the coming school year.

Sometimes there may be touchy subjects or difficult politics that could be uncomfortable for the departing head. Those areas can be smoothed (or at least addressed) by your board chair (or transition committee chair, if different) so that the matter does not poison the relationship between the two heads.

Meetings with top administrators can be productive, and transition visits are important opportunities for relationship building. These are generally not big group meetings with lots of fanfare but quiet, thoughtful discussions about the next few months. If there are critically important donors, the transition visit provides an opportunity for an initial face-to-face visit with them.

The new head should be reminded that faculty, administration, and others may try hard to lobby their new leader during these visits. The new head should not commit to anything during these conversations unless 100 percent sure about it.

THE HEAD OF SCHOOL'S GOALS

An important collaborative exercise for the transition committee, especially with the board chair's involvement, is the development of your new head's goals. With the support of the transition team and in tandem with your board leadership, your new head can start to draft a vision for entry and for the first academic year.

A limited number of clearly stated objectives can help define your new head's priorities and help ensure a strong partnership—and mutual accountability—with the board. Although a draft of goals developed by your new head can serve as a starting point for refinement, committee members must limit their input so that the objectives reflect your new head's leadership style.

Professional development for the new head

A professional development schedule, planned and budgeted well in advance, ensures that the right components are included and that scheduling conflicts are avoided. While a full range of topics should be included in the professional development plans, the emphasis will depend on your new head's previous experience and expertise. As noted in the previous chapter, one highly recommended experience for first-time heads is the NAIS Institute for New Heads. The institute covers a broad range of topics and matches your incoming head with a cohort of new heads across the country. Additional professional development opportunities with regional associations may also help your new head establish relationships in the area.

THE TRANSITION TEAM'S ESSENTIAL GROUNDWORK

The transition committee is in a wonderful position to introduce your incoming head to the culture and rich history of your school and formulate a healthy working relationship between your board leadership and your new head. There is a great deal to do before your new head of school starts. It should be considered a best practice to have a well-established committee providing essential planning, orientation, and reflection.

1. Remember the importance of celebrating your outgoing head of school. A graceful departure is vital to a smooth succession.

2. Make sure your incoming head of school is active in the planning and leadership of the transition process to encourage the proper mindset about school leadership. This can also ensure that the individual is getting all the information a new head really needs and not just what others might (mistakenly) *think* is needed.

3. Clearly define the role of the board versus the role of the transition committee to avoid confusion.

4. Consider one or two transition visits to help pass the baton between the two heads.

5. Consider making the members of the transition team partners in developing the new head's goals, which will later be presented to the full board.

19

Cementing the Partnership Between Board Chair and Head

By Anthony G. Featherston IV

■ Thinking carefully about board succession can do much to ensure the new head's success for years to come.

An old leadership cliché compares the relationship between the head of school and the board chair to a marriage. While clichés can make us dismissive of the underlying message, there is often a kernel of truth to them, and that is certainly the case here. Like many successful marriages, the head-chair relationship, when working optimally, benefits from trust, open communication, some division of labor, and shared ownership—and the primary beneficiaries are the children.

Where the analogy breaks down is around the transition to a new partner. Although the strongest marriages last forever, the healthiest schools benefit from orderly and periodic transitions to new partnerships.

Some schools do not limit how long a board chair may serve, and the new head and current board chair could serve together for many years. But it is more typical that your school will have to appoint a new board chair within the first few years of a head's tenure. Your head's relationship with the new board chair is no less important than the relationship with the first board chair, but typically much less thought goes into it. Why should that be the case? What if the board looked at a head's transition as a four- to six-year process and approached board succession accordingly?

TWO BASIC MODELS

Two primary responsibilities of your board are to ensure the long-term well-being of the school and to support the head of school, which makes the transitions between the board chair and new head especially critical. Few things make or break a headship like the head-chair relationship. A strong partnership can mean great things for your school; a strained one can spell disaster. When a new head is hired, much thought and care are generally given to building this relationship.

There are as many partnership models as there are schools, but most schools typically follow one of two: The current board chair stays on to provide stability; or the head of the search committee, who presumably has already established a solid connection with the incoming head, starts as board chair when the head arrives. In either case, the two must develop a trusting relationship, although it may evolve differently depending on which model is followed.

- **When the current board chair stays on**, continuity is built in. The rest of the community—board, parents, faculty, alumni—can feel confident that the board is being guided by a leader with a proven history at the school. The new head has the opportunity to step into the role with the help of an experienced partner. This can give the new head the time and space to get to know the community without causing ongoing initiatives to lose momentum. A transition committee made up largely of members of the search committee may also help smooth the onboarding process and leverage relationships built during the search. Involving search committee members in this way may also provide more opportunities to grow future board leadership.

- **When the head of the search committee becomes chair**, the school has an opportunity to build on the relationship developed during the search. Presumably, there is a measure of trust and excitement that can serve the head and board well and that can energize the entire school community. In this case, a transition committee made up of both experienced board members and members of the search committee may be preferable. Supporting the head with people who are excited about change but also familiar with the history and traditions of the school can provide a solid foundation as the head settles into place in the first year.

Whatever path a school chooses, usually there is plenty of thoughtful and purposeful preparation given to this transition, which is as it should be. It only makes sense that boards should look beyond that first year or two and that first board chair when planning a new head's entry.

SUCCESSION PLANNING

In addition to ensuring that a school has the proper leader, self-perpetuating boards are also responsible for thoughtful succession planning. If we believe that the head-chair relationship is critical, that onboarding a new head is a years-long process, and that a board must also be intentional about its own leadership succession, isn't there tremendous benefit to thinking of all three together from the start of a new head's tenure? But, of course, there can be challenges as well.

Potential benefits

- **Long-range agenda.** Whatever strategic initiatives are on a board's long-range agenda—building, growth, a campaign, etc.—they can all benefit from forethought. A clear plan of succession to your second board chair as your new head is being appointed helps ensure stability, consistency of vision, and clear communication of priorities. In short, it improves the likelihood of success.

- **Focus on mission.** Board chair succession planning can help your board and head stay mission-focused. Knowing who will be board chair for the first four to six (or more) years of your head's tenure can help ensure consistency of vision and the mission-appropriateness of initiatives.

- **Relationship building.** Think again about the marriage analogy. Knowing the second board chair could be like having a long engagement; it provides the head with the opportunity to build a relationship with the next board chair from day one, even while establishing firm footing with the current board chair. It could even bring a third person into the thought partnership.

- **Stability.** Change makes people nervous. All schools, whether strong and steady, in crisis, or somewhere in between, benefit from stability. So do all members of a school community. A new head can make faculty, parents, alumni, and even students wonder about the direction of the school. A statement by the board about having predictable, long-term board leadership can help calm all constituent groups.

Potential challenges

- A preordained succession plan may turn off otherwise interested and appropriate candidates for the board chair job.

- For any number of reasons, what seems like a good match when a head is hired may not be a few years out. Leadership styles and priorities may be different, or personalities simply may not mesh.

- Once in place, the head may identify someone else on the board as a stronger partner, potentially resulting in hard feelings if a change is made.

- It is not always obvious who the next board chair should be. It does not make sense to force a succession plan if a clear successor is not apparent.

Most of these challenges can be mitigated by delaying the identification of the next board chair by less than a year, allowing enough time for the head and chair to understand the board's political landscape, personality matches, and talent pool. If this transition can be made more predictable, the disruption of the partnership is reduced, and the school is virtually assured of continued smooth operation through the head's first "remarriage."

SERVING A STRATEGIC PURPOSE

The identification, recruitment, hiring, onboarding, and ongoing support of the head of school is critical to the success of the head and, by extension, of the school itself. How this process is laid out and how far into the future a board plans will most likely have significant impact on the head's tenure. At the very least, boards should consider whether a clear succession plan from the beginning—or at least early in the tenure—serves a strategic purpose and, if so, how to put that plan in place for the long-term good of the school.

1. Whether the board chair is in place during the new head search or the future board chair is heading the search committee, think about the transition to a new board chair from the start of the new head's tenure.

2. Consider the school head's transition as a four- to six-year process, and approach board succession accordingly.

3. Consider the balance between stability and flexibility when deciding when to devise a clear plan of succession.

4. Don't force a succession plan if there is no clear successor in place.

5. Be sure that the head has a voice in transition planning, even early on, as it is critical that the head-chair relationship be mutually supportive.

Lay the foundation for good head-board relations.
Ensure that at least through your new head's third year, key trustees with institutional memory of the search are still serving on the board. Board succession planning is a critical component of the search.

Harriet DiCicco, Associate, Educational Directions, Inc.

Be ready for next time by preparing for the expense of search. One approach is to continuously budget a portion of the expected search expense, say 20 percent annually, to build a reserve, thus relieving the pressure on the budget in the year when the expenses occur.

Marc Levinson, Principal, Independent School Solutions, and former Executive Director of Mid-South Independent School Business Officers (MISBO)

Remember: Everything is going to be *just fine*. Searches can start off as such charged, nerve-wracking events—sometimes the committee convinces itself that it's on the verge of Armageddon and, without swift action, the school will be pulled straight into the abyss. But for most schools, the institution is larger than the head, the board, or any particular search. As long as your committee acts with integrity, you're most likely going to end up with a good result.

Devereaux McClatchey, President, Carney, Sandoe & Associates

20

Succession Planning for Next Time

By Siri Akal Khalsa

> ■ Succession planning means both developing a planning mindset and creating a written plan to make sure your school will have an orderly transition when, inevitably, the next leadership change occurs.

"Fail to plan? Plan to fail."

That familiar adage is a powerful reminder that, like any other important project, a successful search for a head of school begins with a well-thought-out plan. Ideally developed well in advance of either a sudden or an anticipated change, a leadership succession plan serves as two things: a framework for thinking about your school's future leadership and a guide for your board as it attends to securing the school's next leader and ensuring continuity.

Systematic planning for the inevitable leadership change has never been more important. A 2009 NAIS study of school leadership and governance reported that 68 percent of sitting heads were planning to retire or change jobs by 2019.[1] The competition among schools for qualified heads who can provide the next generation of leadership is strong and growing. At the same time, the rapidly changing educational environment makes it even more important for a board to "get it right" in selecting the head to lead the school through new, and often uncertain, times.

The tension that arises from the school's need for a leader who can both provide stability and manage change advantageously creates unique opportunities and challenges for your board. Developing a succession plan *before* a leadership change will help the board make better decisions in the search process and avoid the pitfalls that often come with such a change.

Despite the advantages of planning for leadership succession in a thoughtful and strategic way prior to a search, too often the topic doesn't even come up in board discussions until the necessity arises and the urgency is inescapable. The fact is that your school and board will have a greater likelihood of success if you thoroughly and deeply engage in a succession planning process well in advance of the need.

WHAT SUCCESSION PLANNING IS

In its article "Building Leadership Capacity: Reframing the Succession Challenge," the nonprofit Bridgespan Group argues that succession planning is

> not a periodic event triggered by an executive's departure. Instead, it is a *proactive and systematic investment* in building a pipeline of leaders within an organization, so that when transitions are necessary, leaders at all levels are ready to act.[2]

Succession planning means both developing a planning mindset and creating a written plan to ensure the orderly transition of school leadership from your current head to your new leader. The planning mindset is as important as the plan itself because conditions change quickly in schools today. If not regularly reviewed and updated, plans can quickly become stale and irrelevant.

Succession planning rests on three principles:

1. Changes in school leadership are inevitable.
2. No position is more important to the success of a school than its head, so the right match is critical.
3. Identifying, selecting, hiring, and sustaining the school's next head are perhaps the most important tasks a board may have.

With that in mind, your school's leadership succession planning process must address two different circumstances:

1. *Planned leadership change*, when, for example, a sitting head informs your board of a desire to leave the position by a certain date
2. *Unplanned change*, when, for instance, your school head unexpectedly resigns; suddenly has the employment contract terminated; or has an accident, injury, or serious illness that might result in an interruption in leadership

Successfully managing either type of change requires planning that incorporates both "hard" elements, such as budgeting for the expenses associated with a search, and "soft" aspects, such as identifying the ideal qualities the next head will possess.

PLANNED LEADERSHIP SUCCESSION

Everyone is familiar with the advice that the best time to search for a job is when you don't need one. Similarly, the best time for your board to begin succession planning is when it doesn't need to. The board can benefit by taking advantage of the relative calm of the current head's tenure to plan for the school's next leadership, even if that change appears to be years in the future or seems nearly unthinkable. When this type of planning happens before any leadership change, it provides a strong foundation for a search when the time comes and enables the search committee to be much more agile in its work.

At the formal level, succession planning includes these steps:

- Budgeting for the financial resources needed to support the level of search the board anticipates (internal, local, regional, or national; with or without a search consultant)
- Building board consensus on the future direction of the school and on what its ideal state will be in five, 10, and 20 years
- Developing board agreement on the professional and personal qualities the ideal next head of school will possess
- Defining the skills, expertise, attitudes, and understandings the ideal search committee will possess, and ensuring that the board has or will have those people to call on
- Strategic communications planning

Leadership succession planning also requires thorough board-level conversations about these issues:

- The fact that no candidate will possess all desired qualities and how the strategic deficits of the best candidate will be mitigated
- How the strategic deficits your school currently faces will be addressed so that the next head can step onto a platform of strength and not into a minefield of weakness
- The need to support the current head during the transition out
- The need for the sitting head to support the change

- Who will be the board chair in the first year of the new head's tenure
- The possible viability of potential internal candidates
- Identifying and addressing the needs of the school's many constituencies—students, parents, trustees, alumni, community stakeholders—during a time of change

One note of caution: Because leadership succession planning is essentially a strategic plan for the continuity of leadership, it's possible that members of your school community might start to worry that it's a disguised strategy to oust the current leader. Any hint of this type of talk should be dispelled, *early* and *often*. Engaging the current head as a proactive partner in succession planning is one reassuring way to do this.

UNPLANNED CHANGE

There are times when the head of school's tenure is interrupted unexpectedly. Pressing family situations may demand the head's immediate and complete attention; health issues may require short- or long-term leaves; matters may arise that require the sitting head's resignation or, possibly, termination. Any circumstance that significantly interrupts the head's ability to lead has the potential to disrupt normal school operations, unsettle faculty and staff, distance parents, and fracture boards.

Although your board cannot foresee every possible crisis, it can reduce the potential negative impact leadership crises may have by creating a plan that addresses the most probable: short-term leave; long-term leave; and sudden departure due to resignation, termination, or untimely death.

Asking and answering the following questions—in detail and in writing—will give your board the tools it needs to keep the school on course and the community feeling engaged and informed.

1. Who is in charge of the school during a short-term absence of the head of school? Long-term absence?
2. In case of the sudden departure of the head, who will be running the school on a day-to-day basis? How will that person be supported? Compensated?
3. What is the process for communicating headship changes in a way that will sustain the confidence and trust of the different school constituencies?

4. What role will the board, and specifically the executive committee, need to play in order to support the head and the school through the crisis?

Even though it may seem premature to do so, creating this type of "leadership emergency plan" with your new head of school as soon as the individual gets settled in is highly recommended. Schools have crisis management plans that cover almost every circumstance imaginable. Why shouldn't unplanned leadership change be part of that thinking and planning?

THE CASE FOR INTERNAL TALENT DEVELOPMENT

Although "succession planning is the No. 1 organizational concern of U.S. nonprofits," the Bridgespan Group reports, "they are failing to develop their most promising pool of talent: homegrown leaders."[3] In fact, more than 90 percent of independent schools undertake external head of school searches, according to a Heidrick & Struggles report by George Conway and Stephen Miles, "After Success: Replacing a Long-Serving Head of School."[4]

Your board's immediate reaction to filling a headship position might be "national search," but it should weigh the advantages of promoting from within. For one thing, external searches can be expensive. For another, there's always the possibility of losing critical institutional momentum as a head unfamiliar with your school learns the ropes.

Research from the Connecticut Association of Independent Schools (CAIS) supports the strategy of developing internal candidates for the headship. Over a 10-year period, 35 percent of CAIS member schools that recruited and hired externally did not offer those heads a second contract, reports Doug Lyons, CAIS's executive director. During the same decade, all 18 of its schools that hired internal candidates signed those heads on for another term.[5]

This pattern is not exclusive to independent schools. In North America, 55 percent of departing outside CEOs were fired, compared with 34 percent of insiders, according to Ram Charan's still-timely 2005 *Harvard Business Review* article, "Ending the CEO Succession Crisis." In Europe, the split was 70 percent/55 percent.[6]

Sometimes, boards look externally because the school needs a change, and bringing in someone from outside the trenches is the best way to accomplish that. But often it's because, on the surface, there seem to be no suitable internal candidates.

Developing such an internal pipeline, however, is something your board should discuss—and then broach thoughtfully with the current head. In a non-threatening manner, your board can work to help your head understand that succession planning is a hallmark of good governance and not a veiled attempt at replacement.

Your school might also consider making "potential for school leadership" part of the hiring criteria and evaluation process for assistant or associate heads of school, academic directors, and other senior administrators. Mentorship opportunities and the possibility of being groomed for school leadership can make an administrative position more attractive for millennials who are looking for tangible paths to advancement in their careers.

POTHOLES AND POSSIBILITIES

Sally Powell, then head of The Baldwin School (PA), and her board chair, Terry Steelman, wrote in the March/April 2015 *Trustee's Letter*:

> Transitions in our schools can be disruptive, drama-inducing, and difficult to direct. They can also be energizing, enriching, and easy to embrace. When change is in the air, a school must be very purposeful, focused on reinforcing the relationships that bind its broad constituencies.[7]

Your board must also be on the lookout for possible challenges along the way. In a recent conversation with the author, head search consultant Bob Fricker noted that succession-planning efforts can be undermined by heads who are insecure in their positions, weak or confused boards with high trustee turnover, a change-resistant culture, faculty and staff who are overly comfortable with the status quo, and an unexamined and uncorrected pattern of high turnover in the head's office.[8]

For almost all school heads and their boards, the reality is that the *urgent* always overwhelms the *important*. The day-to-day, week-to-week, month-to-month focus that heads and boards invariably take to ensure the short-term survival of the school often precludes planning to maintain strength as leadership transitions.

But it is vital to devote time and attention to the long-term health and success of a school—which includes ongoing succession planning. Your school should create time for it by including it on board meeting agendas and perhaps by making it a generative topic for the board's next retreat.

"The future cannot be predicted, but it can be invented," Dennis Gabor, the

Nobel Prize-winner in physics, wrote in his 1963 book, *Inventing the Future*.[9] Similarly, you cannot predict the future for your school, but you can shape it by addressing leadership succession thoughtfully. Change is inevitable, and it can be disruptive. How successfully your school adapts to demographic shifts, manages economic swings, and adjusts to cultural tides depends largely on the strength and continuity of leadership.

Count on it. Better still, plan for it.

ENDNOTES

[1] National Association of Independent Schools, "The State of Independent School Leadership 2009: Report of Survey Research Among School Heads and Administrators," (unpublished), 2010.

[2] The Bridgespan Group, "Building Leadership Capacity: Reframing the Succession Challenge," 2011; online at https://www.bridgespan.org/insights/library/leadership-development/building-leadership-capacity.

[3] Libbie Landles-Cobb, Kirk Kramer, and Katie Smith Milway, "The Nonprofit Leadership Development Deficit," *Stanford Social Innovation Review*, October 22, 2015; online at https://ssir.org/articles/entry/the_nonprofit_leadership_development_deficit.

[4] George E. Conway and Stephen A. Miles, "After Success: Replacing a Long-Serving Head of School: Ten Myths That Stand in the Way," Heidrick and Struggles; online at https://www.independenteducation.org/File%20Library/Unassigned/George-Conway---After-Success-Final.pdf.

[5] Doug Lyons, personal communication with the author, September 2016.

[6] Ram Charan, "Ending the CEO Succession Crisis," *Harvard Business Review*, February 2005; online at https://hbr.org/2005/02/ending-the-ceo-succession-crisis.

[7] Sally Powell and Terry Steelman, *The Trustee's Letter*, March/April 2015, p. 1.

[8] Bob Fricker, personal communication with the author, June 2016.

[9] Dennis Gabor, *Inventing the Future* (London: Secker & Warburg, 1963).

1. Recognize that succession planning can help your school set itself up for a successful future and, at the same time, avoid the disruption that often accompanies changes in leadership.

2. Keep in mind that what you need to plan for depends on your circumstances. You're likely to experience greater stability in the head's office when you hire from within. But if you need a change of direction, you should probably plan for an external search.

3. Begin planning today by having your board discuss what kind of

leadership the school will need in five to 10 years; ensuring that your school provides career paths that can prepare internal candidates for the headship; and putting money in each year's budget to support a successful search and transition when the time comes.

4. Make sure your planning addresses the most probable types of unexpected change: short-term leave; long-term leave; and sudden departure due to resignation, termination, or untimely death.

Appendices

NAIS Principles of Good Practice

PRINCIPLES OF GOOD PRACTICE FOR HEAD SEARCHES

Overview: The following principles of good practice are designed to help independent schools and their search committees as they embark upon the task of selecting a school head. They are intended to further the likelihood of a professional and fair process that is the foundation for the successful hiring of a new head of school.

Principles of Good Practice: School Search Committees

1. Prior to the formation of the search committee, the board chair appoints a small subcommittee of trustees for gathering information and resources (such as the *NAIS Head Search Handbook* and these NAIS Principles of Good Practice) to identify properly the appropriate approach to the head of school search in light of the school's finances, culture, and other characteristics, paying particular attention to forming a search committee, hiring a search consultant, and diversifying the pool of candidates it seeks.

2. Using the background resources, the search committee devises a search process, communicated to the community at large, a process that is fair, inclusive, and orderly and that adheres to local, state, and federal laws and regulations, including those regarding nondiscrimination in employment. The board of trustees examines how the plan addresses sensitive issues related to confidentiality, inclusivity, and the school's receptivity to change when approving the process recommended by the search committee.

3. The search committee communicates to candidates its protocols, process, and schedule, and the care it will take to ensure a search process that is viewed by candidates as fair, orderly, inclusive, and confidential.

4. While a search consultant or subset of the committee will screen files for appropriateness and will make every effort to present the school with a finalist pool that is both highly qualified in terms of the search committee's criteria and diverse in makeup and attributes, the entire search committee is informed about all candidates who have applied.

5. Because candidates have sometimes found their positions in their own schools jeopardized by being candidates at another school, the early stages of a search are conducted in a manner that ensures complete confidentiality, and the finalist stages of reference-checking by the search committee are executed with great care, sensitivity, and consideration of each candidate's wishes.

6. Contracting with a head of school follows IRS rebuttable presumption protocols, ensuring that the school is compensating the new school leader fairly and appropriately.

Principles of Good Practice: Head Search Consultants

The following principles of good practice for search consultants and search firms establish the principled standards for the process and the expectations of professionalism from the search consultants and search firms.

1. The search consultant (or the search committee chair in the absence of a consultant) incorporates into the process, as appropriate, search committee training recommended in the *NAIS Head Search Handbook* and facilitates the search committee's adherence to NAIS Principles Good Practice.

2. In outlining procedures to the search committee prior to entering a written agreement for the services being rendered, the search consultant provides a full written description of services offered, including estimated expenses and fees; makes known the names of other schools for which he or she actively is performing a search for persons to fill a similar position; and limits searches during any given period to a number that will ensure service of high quality to each client school.

3. The search consultant makes every effort to understand the school, its mission, its culture, its tolerance for change, its preferred leadership style, and the nature of the position to be filled.

4. The search consultant makes every effort to present the school with a diverse group of highly qualified candidates. All principles associated with providing equal opportunity are observed in the process.

5. The search consultant sees the school, not the individual candidate, as the primary client.

6. The search consultant respects the confidentiality of each candidate and impresses upon both search committee and candidates the importance of discretion.

7. Both the search consultant and the search committee check candidates' references with great care.

8. The search consultant keeps the search committee fully informed about the progress of the assignment throughout the search and ensures that each candidate is informed appropriately, promptly, and frequently about the status of his or her candidacy.

PRINCIPLES OF GOOD PRACTICE FOR HEADS OF SCHOOL

Overview: The primary responsibility of the head of an independent school is to carry out the school's stated mission. While there are profoundly different ways to accomplish this goal, NAIS offers the following principles as guideposts for all heads engaged in this rewarding, complex job.

Principles of Good Practice

1. The head works in partnership with the board of trustees to establish and refine the school's mission; articulates the mission to all constituencies—students, faculty and staff, parents, alumni/ae, and the community; and supports the mission in working with all constituencies.

2. The head oversees the shaping of the school's program and the quality of life in the school community.

3. The head establishes an effective manner of leadership and appropriately involves members of the administration and faculty in decision-making.

4. The head is responsible for attracting, retaining, developing, and evaluating qualified faculty and staff.

5. The head is accessible, within reason, and communicates effectively with all constituencies.

6. The head is responsible for financial management, maintenance of the physical plant, strategic planning, and fundraising.

7. The head ensures that every element of school life reflects the principles of equity, justice, and the dignity of each individual.

8. The head is alert to his or her role within the broader networks of schools, school leaders, and the community.

9. The head works to ensure that the principles of good practice of all school operations, especially those of admission, marketing, faculty recruitment, and fundraising, demonstrate integrity at all levels of the school.

PRINCIPLES OF GOOD PRACTICE FOR EQUITY AND JUSTICE

Overview: NAIS schools value the representation and full engagement of individuals within our communities whose differences include—but are not limited to—age, ethnicity, family makeup, gender identity and expression, learning ability, physical ability, race, religion, sexual orientation, and socioeconomic status. NAIS welcomes and celebrates the diversity of our member schools. We expect member schools to create and sustain diverse, inclusive, equitable, and just communities that are safe and welcoming for all. We recognize that to do so requires commitment, reflection, deliberate planning and action, and ongoing accountability. The following NAIS Principles of Good Practice for Equity and Justice provide the foundation for such an independent school community.

Principles of Good Practice

1. The school establishes the foundations for its commitment to equity and justice in its defining documents (mission, core value, and/or philosophy statements).

2. The school respects, affirms, and protects the dignity and worth of each member of its community.

3. The board of trustees and the head of school articulate strategic goals and objectives that promote diversity, inclusion, equity, and justice in the life of the school.

4. The school develops meaningful requirements for cross-cultural competency and provides training and support for all members of its community, including the board of trustees, parents, students, and all school personnel.

5. The board of trustees and the head of school keep the school accountable for living its mission by periodically monitoring and assessing school culture and ongoing efforts in admission, hiring, retention, financial aid, and curriculum development.

6. The school works deliberately to ensure that the board of trustees, administration, faculty, staff, and student body reflect the diversity that is present in the rapidly changing and increasingly diverse school-age population in our country.

7. The head of school ensures that diversity initiatives are coordinated and led by a designated individual who is a member of one of the school leadership teams, with the training, authority, and support needed to influence key areas of policy development, decision-making, budget, and management.

8. The school uses inclusive language in all written, electronic, and oral communication.

9. The school adopts a nondiscrimination statement applicable to the administration of all of its programs and policies, in full compliance with local, state, and federal law. That said, the school makes the law the floor—not the ceiling—for establishing itself as a diverse, inclusive, safe, and welcoming community for all students, staff, and families.

B

Overview of the Search Process

Although each school must choose the process that suits its unique culture, here is a general outline of the steps involved. The timing of each step will vary depending on the school's circumstances.

- As the school prepares to announce the departure of the current head, the board of trustees develops a search strategy based on a shared understanding of the school's past, present, and future (Chapter 1).

- The board develops a plan for a needs assessment (Chapter 2) and for informing and involving the school community in critical stages of the search (Chapter 4).

- The board chair or executive committee appoints a search committee chair (Chapter 3).

- The board and search chair decide on the makeup of the search committee (Chapter 3); whom to appoint as the interim head of school, if appropriate (Chapter 5); and whether to hire a search consultant (Chapter 6). Before the search goes public, the board also approves a broad compensation range (Chapter 16).

- The search committee develops a position description that reflects the school's strategic needs (Chapter 7). The position description is posted in various locations, including ones designed to ensure a diverse candidate pool (Chapters 8-10).

- The search committee develops a pool of initial candidates. Throughout the evaluation and interview process, the committee balances the need for a diverse pool with the imperative to avoid considering characteristics or questions prohibited under federal, state, or local laws (Chapters 8-11).

- The search committee interviews semifinalist candidates. The pool continues to narrow as the committee invites a few finalists to visit the school and meet constituents (Chapters 11-14).

- The search committee recommends a finalist candidate to the board, and the board votes. (Alternatively, the committee may bring forward more than one candidate, and the board makes a deciding vote.) References and background checks are performed. These may be done with the final candidate only or with the final two candidates if the committee or board would like that information as part of its final deliberations (Chapter 15).

- The board appoints a committee to negotiate the final terms and contract. Once the contract is signed, the board receives a final report on the contract terms (Chapter 16).

- The board chair announces the new head, and the transition to new leadership begins. School leaders plan and enact a strategy to announce and launch the head successfully (Chapters 17-20).

Source: Debra P. Wilson, general counsel of NAIS

C

Questions for the Prospective Search Consultant Interview

1. CONSULTANT KNOWLEDGE OF THE SCHOOL

- Why are you interested in working with us on this search?
- What is your process for learning about the school in order to identify candidates who will be a good match?
- What schools strike you as similar to our school? In what ways?
- Are you working with any similar schools currently? If so, how will you handle the possibility of the same candidates in each search?

2. SUCCESS RATE

- What is the average tenure of candidates you've placed in headships?
- What is the shortest tenure? What were the factors that led to the relatively short tenure?

3. THE SEARCH PROCESS

- Describe the search process steps from beginning to end within a timetable that suits our needs.
- Who writes the school profile document intended for prospective candidates? Is that document posted publicly (on the school website, on the consultants' website), or is it a confidential exchange with candidates? To what extent does the profile document candidly outline the current challenges in addition to the opportunities?
- Do your services include bringing the offer to closure? Transition of the new head into the role?

4. THE CANDIDATES

- What is your process for seeking candidates?
- How many applicants would you project for our school? What is a typical number for your searches?
- How do you ensure that the candidate pool is diverse?
- What do you recommend as the best way to manage interest from internal candidates?
- To what extent do you meet all candidates before their materials are presented to the search committee?
- Will the search committee see all dossiers? Does the consultant screen or select before presenting to the search committee?
- Who manages the logistics of the candidates' visits?
- How and when are references checked? Is there a process for checking "unofficial" references?
- How many candidates will the search committee present to the board?
- What do candidates say about your work?

5. THE SEARCH COMMITTEE

- What do you recommend for the composition and size of the search committee?
- How do you recommend we manage constituent participation in the process? Is there a role for faculty? For parents? For students? For alums? For trustees beyond the search committee? Do you recommend the use of advisory committees? Why or why not?
- What are the best qualifications of the search committee chair?

6. COMMUNICATION

- What recommendations do you have for us about communication about the search?
- What processes do you recommend for dealing with the needs of candidates requesting confidentiality?

7. CONSULTANT PRESENCE

- When would you expect to be on campus or with the search committee?

- To what extent do you join the process for interviewing candidates? Do you coach the search committee on positive and appropriate interviewing? If so, at what point in the process?

8. NICHE/DISTINCTIVES

- What distinguishes your firm or work from that of other consultants?

Source: Claudia Daggett, president of the Independent Schools Association of the Central States (ISACS)

Sample Position Description

OPEN PLAINS ACADEMY*
Open Plains, Illinois

HEAD OF SCHOOL

The School

Open Plains Academy (OPA) is a coeducational day school with 750 students in kindergarten through 12th grade. OPA enjoys a long record of community strength and academic excellence. Situated on two nearby campuses, the school's High Street Campus houses the Middle and Upper Schools while the Lower School resides on the Uptown Campus.

Open Plains Academy values its history and tradition, giving credit to its generations of parents, students, and faculty and their dedication to learning and service that are the foundation of the quality and strength of today's school. OPA is a community enriched by a diverse constituency motivated by strong interpersonal relationships, new challenges, and academic excellence. The mission statement for OPA captures this spirit:

> **Open Plains Academy serves a diverse and motivated community of learners by inspiring a lifelong passion for education; promoting balanced intellectual, social, and physical growth; and cultivating creativity, independent thinking, and a commitment to service.**

Today, the school enjoys a national reputation for its academic excellence and merit. Open Plains Academy is distinctive for its sense of community, its experiential education, and its relationships between faculty and students. The OPA experience is centered on the dynamic academic exchange between students and faculty. Guided and supported by administrators, teachers are empowered both to create and design a meaningful course of study that is student-centered and to develop a coherent and linear educational experience for students from kindergarten through 12th

---

*All references to Open Plains School, Sally E. Smith, and other Open Plains constituents in these appendices are fictitious.

grade. Approximately 90 percent of the faculty hold advanced degrees, and more than half have a lengthy tenure with Open Plains Academy. An endowed fund for faculty development and a sabbatical program enable teachers to obtain support for professional enrichment and growth.

Nearly 270 students attend the Lower School program, which encompasses kindergarten through fifth grade. The Lower School focuses on nurturing the whole child and emphasizes an inviting, colorful, and energetic environment in which young children are encouraged to be active in their own learning. Led by experienced and dedicated faculty, classes are organized in team-taught multi-age and single-grade rooms. The spacious Uptown Campus is enhanced by an auditorium, playground, outdoor classroom, garden, and a seasonal skating rink.

Newly constructed on the High Street Campus, the Middle School is designed to meet the educational, developmental, and emotional needs of adolescents. The fully integrated curriculum emphasizes wide-ranging exploration as well as focused attention on skill development in each discipline. Middle School students are encouraged to broaden their intellectual boundaries by participating in athletics and fine arts and to push themselves to achieve their personal best. Beginning in seventh grade, all students—and their teachers—use laptop computers as an integral part of the core curriculum.

The Upper School further emphasizes the educational partnership between faculty and students. With an average class size of 14, OPA students learn how to think for themselves with teachers who are passionate scholars of the subjects they teach. During recent years, Open Plains Academy has incorporated the Harkness Table teaching method in 14 of the Upper School classrooms as a tool to enhance existing classroom relationships between faculty and students and to encourage collaborative learning. At the Harkness table, classmates learn by discussing their questions and ideas rather than solely by taking notes. Teachers are participants in the discussion, guiding students in significant ways without lecturing. Upper School courses center on liberal arts curricula, including language arts, mathematics, science, social studies, and languages such as Chinese, French, and Spanish. Other required courses include technology, fine arts, wellness, visual arts, and physical education. In many respects, the OPA experience is similar to that of a small liberal arts college because of its rich and authentic curricula and ethos. Thus, it is not surprising that graduates of OPA attend highly regarded liberal arts colleges and universities across the United States.

Open Plains Academy operates on a budget of $15 million and is in a strong financial condition. The school's annual fund is $1 million, and its endowment is $29 million. Efforts are currently underway to organize a significant capital campaign for endowment, financial aid, and campus additions and improvements.

Pat Jones, who has served as head of school since 2005, has been appointed head of the Forward Progress School in Baltimore. Under Ms. Jones's leadership, OPA's

OPEN PLAINS ACADEMY
AT A GLANCE

Founded: 1947

Enrollment: 750
Lower School (K-5): 267
Middle School (6-8): 231
Upper School (9-12): 252

Students of Color: 29%

Faculty and Staff: 97

Average Class Size: 12-14

Student-to-Teacher Ratio: 7:1

Tuition:
Lower (K-5): $25,500
Middle (6-8): $27,000
Upper (9-12): $29,500

Financial Aid: $2 million to 24% of students

Budget: $15 million

Endowment and Other Reserves: $29 million

Annual Fund: $1 million

academic program and community have been enriched by the construction of a new Middle School, the reduction of class sizes, the implementation of a laptop computer program, the formation of a diversity plan of action, and the introduction of the Harkness teaching method to the Upper School curriculum.

The Board of Trustees has launched a nationwide search for Ms. Jones's successor. Open Plains Academy will look to the new head to provide strategic vision to the institution and to guide the community as it embarks on a capital campaign and experiences additional growth during the coming years. Challenges for the future include the following:

- Continually evolving academic and curricular programs and ensuring that appropriate infrastructure, systems, and accountabilities are in place to maintain consistency while honoring faculty autonomy and the needs of individual students

- Increasing various kinds of diversity among students, faculty, administration, and the board, and bringing greater attention to matters of equity and inclusion

- Executing aggressive fundraising plans for a major campaign and significant growth in the annual fund and major gifts

- Making improvements to both campuses through construction of a new performing arts building and athletic field house as well as renovating the gymnasium, dining hall, science rooms, and athletic fields

Responsibilities

The head of school will report to the board of trustees and will be accountable for the academic quality and institutional strength of Open Plains Academy. He or she will be responsible for leading and binding together the multiple constituencies that make OPA a vital and compelling institution by preserving the school's culture and traditions while embracing the future. The head will ensure that Open Plains Academy's administrative policies are appropriate to the needs of the school. Specific duties will include the following:

- Working closely with trustees and other key constituents on the school's strategic direction, campus improvement plans, and institutional advancement

- Continuing the school's tradition of providing a student-centered and supportive atmosphere in which faculty and students act in partnership to achieve academic and individual successes

- Guiding educational policy and refining OPA's academic, arts, and athletic offerings in order to maintain and enhance the school's high level of educational excellence

- Managing the school on a day-to-day basis by empowering faculty and staff through delegation of responsibility and authority while retaining ultimate accountability

- Recruiting, developing, and retaining an outstanding faculty and staff who are committed to professional development and lifelong learning

- Maintaining fair, firm, and consistently applied administrative and disciplinary policies and procedures

- Serving as a key advocate and leader in Open Plains Academy's continued efforts in the areas of diversity, equity, inclusion, and cultural competence

- Creating and managing budgets and financial plans and, in collaboration with the Finance Committee and the chief financial officer, otherwise maintaining the short- and long-term fiscal health of the school

Candidate Qualities

Leadership

- A person who leads by active and visible involvement in the total life of the school

- A leader whose vision, clarity of thought, and base of knowledge lead him or her to establish ambitious goals, to create passion for and inspire involvement with the school, and to articulate compellingly the institution's objectives

- An individual who leads through a balance of motivation and discipline, vision and practicality, and a sense of urgency and patience

- A role model who embodies and reflects a strong moral character, commitment to academic excellence, and respect for others in all aspects of his or her life

Experience

- At least seven years as a senior administrator in an independent school setting, ideally with exposure to multiple grades and divisions

- A background that demonstrates the ability to lead organizations through transformation and continuous improvement

- Experience with fiscal management, institutional advancement, admissions, and establishing school policies

- A successful track record of attracting, empowering, and retaining a highly qualified and diverse staff of teachers who impart knowledge, love of learning, and self-confidence

Skills and Knowledge

- A highly refined sense of organizational dynamics and how they must be deftly guided in order to accomplish the mission of the school

- Ability to set and affirm boundaries while championing a sense of community and mutual concern

- Strong public speaking and writing skills, including the ability to communicate concepts and ideas effectively to a wide range of constituents

- The business and management expertise necessary to develop strategic plans, to install and improve administrative infrastructures, and to prepare school budgets and schedules

Personal Traits

- Comfortable professionally and socially in an environment that values a high degree of both formal and informal communication and interaction between the head and the school's many constituents

- A disciplined, patient, and unflappable person who brings understanding and perspective to bear on difficult issues while exhibiting grace under pressure

- A culturally competent leader whose demonstrated commitment to fostering a diverse and inclusive community serves as an inspiration to others

- A person open to various points of view while having the courage of conviction and decisiveness necessary to advocate on behalf of OPA's mission and values

Other Considerations

Compensation	Highly competitive among comparable NAIS schools.
Location	Open Plains, Illinois
Website	www.openplainsacademy.org
Travel	Minimal
Education	Master's degree required

Source: Linc Eldredge, president of Brigham Hill Consultancy

E

Sample Reference Questions

As your search committee moves semifinalists to the finalist stage, you must engage in thorough reference checking. Assure those providing references that the conversations will be confidential, and have a set of questions that will be asked of all candidates as well as questions that are specific to individual candidates. Push for specificity about ways in which the candidates were and weren't—successful.

SAMPLE GENERAL REFERENCE QUESTIONS

- How do you see this candidate's readiness for headship?
- What are this person's strengths?
- Give an example of a complex project this person has overseen and how he or she managed it.
- Describe the individual's level of organization and follow-through.
- Talk about a time when there was strong disagreement about a direction the candidate wanted to pursue and how this person managed that disagreement.
- Talk about faculty interactions. Peer interactions. Student interactions. Parent interactions.

SAMPLE SPECIFIC REFERENCE QUESTIONS

- In our interview, the candidate talked about her struggle with parents about the math program. What is your perception of this, and how did she handle the disagreements that occurred?
- We found the candidate quite articulate when talking about curriculum and students but less so when speaking about fundraising and finance. Yet he is currently involved with those areas as your head of school. Talk about how you and fellow board members view his financial competence.
- Drawing from the candidate's years as admission director at your school, talk

about the specific ways she developed new marketing strategies, used both print and digital media, and opened new markets.

Source: Bruce Shaw, Independent Consultant

F

Sample Term Sheet*

**SALLY E. SMITH
HEAD OF SCHOOL
OPEN PLAINS ACADEMY**

DESCRIPTION	PROPOSED TERMS
Position	Head of School, reporting to the Board of Trustees
Term of Employment	Three (3) years
Start Date	July 1, 20XX
Renewal/Extension	The parties shall meet by no later than June 30, 2020, to discuss the renewal, extension, or nonrenewal of the employment agreement.
Compensation	
Initial Base Salary	$250,000; base salary will be subject to annual increase equal to the percentage increase to the Consumer Price Index for the Chicago metropolitan area as of March of the year preceding the budget year, plus an additional increase at the Board's discretion in consideration of compensation increases for the school's senior staff.
Standard Benefits	
Retirement Plan	Benefits as provided for other employees of the school subject to the compensation limits of the Internal Revenue Code; pursuant to the terms of the retirement plan, Ms. Smith is required to contribute at least 5 percent of base salary in order for the school to contribute 10 percent of base salary to the 403(b) plan.

*Actual contractual terms will differ from school to school.

Group Medical/Dental/Vision	Benefits as provided for other employees of the school
Life Insurance	Same benefit as provided for other employees of the school; current benefit provides for term life coverage with a death benefit equal to the base salary of the employee but subject to a maximum benefit of $200,000.
Long-term Disability Insurance	Same benefit as provided for other employees of the school
Executive Benefits	
457(f) Plan	The school shall annually credit 2.5 percent of then-current base salary as of each June 30 of the Term to a deferred compensation plan on Ms. Smith's behalf under Section 457(f) of the Internal Revenue Code, beginning June 30, 2019; all accrued credits to the Plan shall vest and be payable to Ms. Smith upon the earliest to occur of her completion of the Term of the Agreement, her termination without cause, her disability, or her death; if Ms. Smith's employment is terminated for cause or she voluntarily resigns from employment, she shall have no rights to payments from the 457(f) plan.
Membership Dues	The school will pay the annual dues and membership fees of organizations of benefit to facilitate Ms. Smith's duties, including membership in state, regional, and national organizations of independent schools. The payment of such expenses shall be subject to prior approval of the board chair.
Parking	The school will provide a parking space at or near the school's main office for Ms. Smith's use.
Legal Fees	The school will pay 50 percent of Ms. Smith's legal fees incurred in the negotiation and drafting of this term sheet and her employment agreement, up to a maximum of $2,500 of her total legal fees.

Other Benefits	
Vacation Leave	Twenty (20) business days of vacation leave per year; in addition to regular school vacation days during the academic year. Accrual of unused vacation leave and treatment upon termination of employment shall be determined in accordance with the school's policies for all employees.
Holidays and Discretionary Days	As provided by the school's policies for all employees
Business and Travel Expenses	Reimbursement of all reasonable school-related business and travel expenses; Ms. Smith shall be eligible to travel business class on flights of more than six (6) hours but shall first apply any available mileage upgrades; said expenses to be reviewed every six months by the chair of the board or his/her designee who does not report to Ms. Smith.
Spousal Travel	School will pay up to $5,000 per year for the travel expenses of Ms. Smith's spouse.
Termination without Cause/Severance	School may terminate without cause upon thirty (30) days' written notice; payout may be for up to one (1) year upon termination, subject to execution of a general release by Ms. Smith in favor of the school. Ms. Smith shall receive continued payment of her then-existing base salary for up to twelve (12) months from the date of termination. School shall also pay for COBRA coverage during this time. Ms. Smith shall have an obligation to mitigate school expenses during this time by seeking new employment. In the event that new employment does not include a salary of the same or greater amount than Ms. Smith's original salary at the school, school shall continue to pay the difference.
Resignation	Ms. Smith to provide the school at least six (6) months' written notice; Ms. Smith shall not be entitled to any further compensation or benefits beyond the effective date of termination of employment.

Participation on Corporate Boards and Outside Activities	Ms. Smith to obtain prior approval from the chair of the board to serve on any for-profit or nonprofit boards; Ms. Smith will not provide services for compensation to any other entity during her employment by the school.

AGREED TO:

Date _____ For the School_____

Date _____ Sally E. Smith_____

Source: Debra Wilson, general counsel of NAIS

G

Sample Transition Timetable

LATE FALL TO DECEMBER

Given the nature of the head of school search cycle, some schools may begin their transition in the late fall. It is important not to accelerate the entire transition timeline, especially the public aspects beyond the initial announcement. Heads-elect will need time to conclude their service at their current schools, and the hiring schools need to properly honor their departing heads of school.

JANUARY TO JUNE

- Complete contract.
- Sign head-elect up for NAIS's Institute for New Heads (if head-elect is new to headship).
- Develop communications plan:
  - Distribute announcement.
  - Develop press release/magazine article.
- Plan and execute farewell and celebration for current head.
- Assemble transition committee:
  - Be certain housing is arranged and spouse/partner is introduced to job possibilities, if desired.
  - Help children in school placement.
  - Assist in moving details.
  - Plan help with learning about local living details (grocery, cleaners, doctors, etc.).
  - Plan fall school and community activities of introduction.
  - Plan convocation/installation for new head.
- Have head-elect visit school several times (two trips are recommended, and events should be selected carefully from the list below):
  - Introduce head-elect to important constituents.
  - Have head-elect meet with current head.
  - Have head-elect meet with transition committee.
  - Have head-elect meet briefly with full faculty.

  – Have head-elect meet briefly with trustees.
- Have board chair and head-elect plan review of the following:
  – Current strategic objectives
  – Accreditation report
  – Historical perspectives on management structure/major events
  – Board goals, composition, schedule, committee charges and goals
  – Budget
  – Process for goal setting and evaluation for head

JULY TO FALL

- Be sure head and family have vacation time after their move and before school begins.
- If new to headship, head-elect should attend the NAIS Institute for New Heads.
- Assist head in finding and retaining a mentor or executive coach, if new to headship.
- Introduce head to school community:
  – Summer meetings with administrators
  – Late summer/early fall individual meetings with faculty
  – Shadow classes at each grade level
  – Attend opening parent meetings
  – Plan alumni meetings and travel
- Plan events for head to get to know trustees, and have trustees introduce head to wider community.
- Arrange meetings for head with important supporters of the school.
- Arrange meetings for head with town and neighborhood officials.
- Establish regular meetings with board chair:
  – Finalize head's goals for year and evaluation process.
  – Keep open channels of communication.
- Have fall convocation/installation.

FIRST YEAR

- Support new head as the individual gets to know the school community.
- Give head time to build trust before setting long-term goals.

Source: Jerry Larson, managing partner of Educational Directions, Inc.; compiled from various school searches

Sample Head of School Announcement

To the Open Plains Community:

It with great pleasure that I announce that the Board of Trustees of the Open Plains Academy has selected Sally E. Smith to become our next head of school, effective July 1, 20XX. We chose Sally from a national pool of impressive candidates after a very thorough search process in which all of our community's constituencies were engaged.

This unanimous appointment comes with the whole-hearted support of our OPA Head Search Committee. In Sally, we have found a vibrant educator who possesses the creativity, commitment, and vision to build on the energetic leadership provided by Pat Jones, who will become head of the Forward Progress School in Baltimore.

Sally currently serves as head of Yellow Hills School, a K-12 day school in suburban Chicago (675 students; 85 faculty and staff). Originally from North Dakota, Sally graduated from high school in Fargo and earned her bachelor's degree at Beloit College and her master's in educational leadership and policy analysis at the University of Wisconsin. Before joining Yellow Hills in 2012, she served in independent schools as a math teacher, department head, lower and upper school dean, and field hockey coach.

At Yellow Hills, Sally's collaborative leadership style and in-depth knowledge of the challenges independent education faces helped the school undertake several strategic initiatives. She guided an overhaul of the curriculum, led the upper school to introduce the Harkness teaching method, oversaw the introduction of several technological innovations, steered improvements to the physical plant, and spearheaded a successful effort to increase the diversity of the school's student body and faculty. She also used her strong financial, talent management, and marketing skills to help Yellow Hills increase both its enrollment and its endowment.

Above all, Sally brings a passion for student-centered education and a strong respect for the value of inspired teaching by empowered faculty. As one OPA parent observed after meeting her, "You can't miss her enthusiasm for young people of all ages—her eyes lit up whenever she spoke of the importance of learning and the fun of being around students and teachers."

We are also pleased to welcome Sally's husband, Tim, and their 12-year-old twins, Katelyn and Connor, who are planning to enroll at OPA. Tim is an accountant. Sally's interests include hiking, visiting national parks, cheering for Chicago sports teams, and cooking and eating with her family.

In accepting her appointment, Sally said:

> Having long been aware of Open Plains Academy's reputation for educational excellence, I could not be more thrilled to be selected as its next head of school. It is a particular honor to follow Pat Jones, whose role in creating a diverse and motivated community of learners is so inspiring to me. I am eager to build on that foundation as I collaborate with the accomplished faculty, staff, and board to prepare our students and school for a world full of both challenges and opportunities. Everyone I've met has made me feel excited about OPA's enormous potential. I look forward to working with everyone in this dynamic community to preserve its culture and traditions while embracing its future.

Sincere thanks are due to the members of the Head Search Committee, who worked tirelessly throughout this months-long search. We are also grateful for the invaluable support of our Board of Trustees. In addition, we appreciate the wise counsel of Alex Carter and Jean Berg of our search firm, Lee & Associates.

In addition, I want to express my deep gratitude to our faculty, staff, administrators, students, parents, and alumni. What a wonderful community we have! Your deep insights into OPA's past, present, and future were indispensable in helping us identify the kind of leader we need. In addition, your enthusiastic welcome made Sally and all our visiting candidates see why our school is justifiably proud of a warm and friendly community.

After benefiting from Pat Jones's outstanding leadership, we knew when we undertook this search that getting it right was vitally important. I am confident that Sally is the right leader for our school's next chapter, just as I'm optimistic that our entire community will thrive in the years to come. We look forward to welcoming her and her family.

Sincerely,
Chris Gordon
Chair, Board of Trustees
Co-chair, Head Search Committee

Source: Compiled from various school sources

I

Sample Charge and First-year Goals for a New Head of School

CHARGE TO HEAD OF SCHOOL SALLY E. SMITH

from the Open Plains Academy Board of Trustees
August 20XX

1. Working closely with the trustees, faculty, staff, students, parents, and alumni of Open Plains Academy, bring educational leadership in support of the mission of the school. Provide energy and direction to a community that is passionate about providing a student-centered and supportive atmosphere in which faculty and students are partners in achieving success. Enhance mutual trust and respect, which are foundational principles of strong institutions.

2. Learn about and appreciate the identity and quality of the school. These include the K-12 structure that ensures strong academic and cultural traditions rooted in the youngest children and strengthened over 13 years, the cultural and personal diversity that enlivens the school community, and the lifelong passion for education that characterizes our mission.

3. As chief spokesperson for the academy, convey OPA's goals and values to all constituencies, including students, faculty, staff, alumni, and parents. Promote the academic mission of the academy and our commitment to developing balanced intellectual, social, and physical growth as well as a commitment to service.

4. Move forward several key initiatives that are already underway, and direct the ongoing efforts that sustain OPA's identity and strength:

   • Enroll academically talented students from all backgrounds.

   • Ensure that we have appropriate infrastructure, systems, and accountabilities in place to maintain consistency while honoring faculty autonomy and individual students' needs.

   • Prepare for a capital campaign.

- Work with the board, administration, faculty, and staff to develop a plan for broad-based strategic action regarding the school's direction, improvement plans, finances, and institutional advancement.

- Oversee completion of the new performing arts building and athletic field house as well as plans to renovate the gymnasium, dining hall, science rooms, and athletic fields.

- Recruit, retain, and energize an outstanding faculty and staff committed to professional development and lifelong learning.

- Support and enhance the school's continued efforts in the areas of diversity, equity, inclusion, and cultural competence.

- Manage physical and financial resources to meet priorities in faculty compensation, financial aid, renovating and preserving physical assets, and addressing needs that develop as a result of improved programming.

Source: Compiled from various school sources

About the Contributors

ABOUT THE EDITOR

Vince Watchorn, editor of *The NAIS Head Search Handbook*, is head of the Providence Country Day School (RI). He has played a role in more than 10 head of school searches and transitions, including as search committee chair, transition committee chair, and communications coordinator. A graduate of the Tatnall School (DE), he serves as a faculty member of the NAIS Institute for New Heads and lead faculty of the NAIS Fellowship for Aspiring School Heads. He is a trustee of West Nottingham Academy (MD) and the Penland School of Crafts (NC).

ABOUT THE AUTHORS

Jane Armstrong is a founder and managing partner of Independent Thinking, an independent school executive search firm. Her career in schools included teaching, coaching, and serving as a dean of students and a director of development. She has also served as a school trustee.

Christopher B. Arnold is a founder and senior partner of Educational Directions, Inc., a search consulting and publishing firm in Portsmouth, Rhode Island.

Thomas J. Banks is head of school at West Nottingham Academy (MD). In addition to serving as a teacher and administrator at the Milton Hershey School (PA), he was head of the upper and middle schools and assistant head of school at Harrisburg Academy (PA).

Caroline G. Blackwell is vice president of equity and justice initiatives at NAIS. Formerly, she served as executive director of the Metro Human Relations Commission in Nashville, Tennessee, and worked at the University School of Nashville for 17 years, including as its director of multicultural affairs.

Kendall R. Cameron was most recently the assistant head of school and associate director of Upper School at Friends Select School (PA). Currently she works with schools on strategic plan and accreditation implementation. She is also president of the board of trustees at West Nottingham Academy (MD).

Charles F. Clark has served as a head of school at eight independent schools over 33 years. At five of those he served as interim head, most recently at the Kingsbury Center (DC). His areas of expertise include board development, startups, strategic planning, and executive coaching.

John E. (Jack) Creeden is head of Chadwick School (CA). In addition to working at the college and university level, he has served as head of three independent schools and president of School Year Abroad. Creeden has presented workshops on board governance, cross-cultural competency, and the intersection between global studies and diversity initiatives in independent schools.

Cris Clifford Cullinan is co-chair of the National Advisory Council for the annual National Conference on Race and Ethnicity in Higher Education (NCORE) and founder of Actual Leadership in Vital Equity (ALIVE). She has been a consultant to schools, colleges, and universities on issues of equity, institutional privilege, and meaningful inclusion for more than 25 years.

Claudia Daggett is the president of the Independent Schools Association of the Central States (ISACS). The recommendations in her chapter are based on interviews with 12 recently placed heads of schools; her time as association executive for ISACS and for the Elementary School Heads Association; and her experience as search consultant with Gregory Floyd & Associates, head of school at Friends Academy (MA), and candidate in several searches.

Linc Eldredge founded Brigham Hill Consultancy, a retained executive search firm specializing in senior-level engagements for independent schools and other nonprofits, after 18 years as a partner with multinational search firms. In addition to his involvement with schools, foundations, cultural institutions, volunteer associations, and other such organizations, he has served on the boards of The Hockaday School (TX), the Chewonki Foundation, and The

Dallas Institute of Humanities and Culture as well as the Committee on Trustees of Dartmouth College.

Anthony G. (Tony) Featherston IV is the head of The Town School (NY). His career has included stints at Concord Academy (MA), Kent Denver School (CO), Pine Point School (CT), and Elmwood Franklin School (NY).

Ayanna Hill-Gill, known as Yanni, is the head of school at Atlanta Girls' School (GA). With more than 20 years of experience in single-gender education and as a graduate of an all-girls' high school, Yanni is passionate about women leadership and girls' education. She serves on the board of the Heads Network and the National Coalition of Girls' Schools as well as the Advisory Board of the Global Village Project, an all-girls' school for refugees in Decatur, Georgia.

Siri Akal Khalsa is executive director of the Northwest Association of Independent Schools (NWAIS). Before joining NWAIS, he served as assistant head, head, and then president of Chapel Hill-Chauncy Hall School (MA) for 14 years. He is also the former director of studies and assistant head of school at Oakwood Friends School (NY).

Jerry Larson is the managing partner and executive coach with Educational Directions, Inc. He is a former two-time head of Cheshire Academy (CT) and Aspire Academy in Doha, Qatar.

Deirdre Ling has been a search consultant with Educators' Collaborative since 2003. After 25 years as dean of admissions, assistant chancellor, and vice chancellor for university relations and development at the University of Massachusetts at Amherst, she transitioned into independent education as the head of Middlesex School (MA), a position she held for 13 years.

John Mackenzie joined Educators' Collaborative as consultant in 2013. Previously, he served as a head of school for 22 years, including six at Worcester Academy (MA) and 16 at Columbus Academy (OH). He has also held senior administrative positions at Belmont Hill School (MA), Milton Academy (MA), and The Potomac School (VA).

Rosa-Lyn Morris is a principal consultant with Korn Ferry's Global Education and Nonprofit Practice in the firm's Washington, DC, office. A former teacher and an educator at heart, she specializes in executive searches for education-related organizations, including K-12 and higher education.

Doreen S. Oleson is a search consultant and executive coach at Resource Group 175. Before joining RG175, she served as head of Saint Mark's School (CA) for 25 years. She has also been president of the governing boards of the National Association of Episcopal Schools and the California Association of Independent Schools.

Thomas P. Olverson is a consultant at Resource Group 175, where he focuses on head of school searches and mentoring school heads. Before joining the firm, he served as head of The Rivers School (MA) for 17 years and Seabury Hall (HI) for 10 years. He writes extensively on independent school leadership issues at www.rg175.com.

Donna Orem is president of NAIS. She speaks and writes frequently about leadership, governance, and trends in independent education. She has served as a trustee for several organizations, including as the chair of one independent school board and vice chair of another.

Amani Reed is head of The School at Columbia University (NY). He has also served at the University of Chicago Laboratory Schools (IL), Lakeside School (WA), and Sewickley Academy (PA). He has played central roles in progressive curriculum development with a focus on equity and justice.

Kim Roberts works at Google developing an applied computer science program for college students to encourage women and other underrepresented groups to enter high-tech careers. Formerly she served as head of Garrison Forest School (MD) and in various advancement and development roles at Castilleja School (CA) and Mark Day School (CA). She co-founded the Young Women Leaders Program, a mentoring program for adolescent girls from underresourced communities, at the University of Virginia.

Laura Ryan Shachoy is a lawyer who specialized in election law early in her career and is currently involved in nonprofit environmental work. She is a longtime trustee at Falmouth Academy (MA) and chaired the school's search for a new head in 2017.

Bruce A. Shaw has taught in and led independent schools for more than 40 years. He was the director of Shady Hill School (MA) for 16 years; before that, he headed Marin Academy (CA) for 10 years. An independent consultant since 2010, he has mentored fellow heads through programs at NAIS and the Association of Independent Schools in New England (AISNE).

Karla Taylor, a longtime contributor to NAIS publications, is the editorial project director of the *NAIS Head Search Handbook*.

Amada Torres is vice president of studies, insights, and research at NAIS. She conducts studies and speaks regularly on issues related to independent education, trends affecting independent schools, financial sustainability, admissions and marketing, and advocacy.

Agnes Underwood is vice president with the Search and Consulting Group of Carney, Sandoe & Associates. She is the former headmistress of the National Cathedral School (DC) and Garrison Forest School (MD). Underwood edited the 2006 edition of *The NAIS Head Search Handbook*.

Debra P. Wilson is general counsel at NAIS. She analyzes regulatory and legal issues related to all aspects of independent schools, develops legal advisories, and oversees NAIS's government relations work. Wilson has served on the boards of three independent schools, including as board chair for one of them.